100 WALKS IN

Gloucestershire

The Crowood Press

First published in 1990 by
The Crowood Press Ltd
Ramsbury
Marlborough
Wiltshire SN8 2HR

Revised edition 1994

British Library Cataloguing-in-Publication Data
A catalogue record for this book is available from the British Library

ISBN 1 85223 827 5

All maps by Philip Smith

Typeset by Carreg Ltd, Nailsea, Bristol

Printed and bound in Great Britain by
Biddles Ltd, Guildford and King's Lynn

The Contributors

Pauline and John Beckett

Molly and Norman Roberts

Keith Salliss

Marion and Maurice Teal

Rose Wordsworth

CONTENTS

North-East

34. Cleeve Cloud and West Down 9m (14.5km)
35. Wold Villages 10m (16km)

North-West

36. Robinswood Hill Country Park 4m (6.5km)
37. Severn Way Path $4^1/_2$m (7km)
38. Prinknash Abbey and Painswick Hill $4^1/_2$m (7km)
39. Deerhurst to Apperley 5m (8km)
40. Flaxley Woods and Welshbury 5m (8km)
41. or including Welshbury $5^1/_2$m (8.5km)
42. Flaxley Woods 4m (6.5km)
43. May Hill to Cliffords Mesne 5m (8km)
44. Around Ashleworth $6^1/_2$m (10km)
45. From Avon to Severn $7^1/_2$m (12km)
46. North West Dean Forest $7^1/_2$m (12km)
47. Kempley and Dymock 8m (13km)
48. Westbury and the Severn's Bank 8m (13km)
49. Highmeadow Wood $8^1/_2$m (13.5km)
50. Symonds Yat Rock to Christchurch 10m (16km)

South-West

51. Tortworth Lake 1m (2km)
52. The River Severn near Shepperdine 3m (5km)
53. Woodmancote and Dursley 3m (5km)
54. Around Lasborough 3m (5km)
55. Wotton Hill and Wotton-under-Edge 4m (6km)
56. Hill and Bevington 4m (6km)
57. Slimbridge to Cambridge 4m (6 km)
58. Uley Village and Shadwell 4m (6km)
59. Selsley and Woodchester 4m (6.5km)
60. Aston Down to Frampton Mansell 4m (6.5km)
61. The Stroudwater Valley, Route 1 4m (6.5km)
62. Alderley and Tresham $4^1/_2$m (7km)
63. The Stroudwater Valley, Route 2 $4^1/_2$m (7km)
64. Toadsmoor Valley 5m (8km)
65. Brookend to Sharpness 5m (8km)

66. Waterley Bottom 5m (8km)
67. East Dean 5m (8km)
68. Cam Peak to Uley Bury $5^1/_2$m (9km)
69. The Tip of the Horseshoe 6m (9.5km)
70. Newark Park and Ozlewoth Bottom $6^1/_2$m (9.5km)
71. Berkeley to Ham $6^1/_2$m (9.5km)
72. South-East Dean Forest $6^1/_2$m (9.5km)
73. North Nibley and Stinchcombe Hill $6^3/_4$m (10.5km)
74. Around Slad 7m (11km)
75. Brockweir to Bigsweir 7m (11km)
76. Nailsworth and Avening 7m (11km)
77. Central Dean Forest 7m (11km)
78. Staunton and Redbrook $7^3/_4$m (12.5km)
79. Dean Forest and Staple Edge $8^1/_2$m (13.5km)
80. Standish and Stockend $8^1/_2$m (13.5km)
81. Harescombe and Haresfield 9m (14.5km)
82. Selsley and Nympsfield 9m (14.5km)
83. The Wye Valley, Brockweir 9m (14.5km)
84. Cranham and Coopers Hill $9^3/_4$m (15.5km)
85. Rodborough and Minchinhampton 10m (16km)
86. Painswick and Sheepscombe 10m (16km)
87. Vale of Berkeley $11^1/_2$m (18.5km)
88. or 14m (22.5km)
89. Frampton-on-Severn 12m (19km)

South-East

90. Hailey Wood and Coates 4m (6.5km)
91. Ablington and Calcot Circular $4^1/_2$m (7km)
92. Fairford River Walk $4^1/_2$m (7km)
93. Miserden Park $5^1/_4$m (8.5km)
94. The Ampneys 6m (9.5km)
95. South Cerney 6m (9.5km)
96. Coln St Aldwyn and Bibury 6m (9.5km)
97. Coln Valley Circular 7m (11km)
98. Sapperton 8m (13km)
99. Coln St Aldwyn and Hatherop 8m (13km)
100. The Duntisbournes and Edgeworth 9m (14.5km)

INTRODUCTION

The Crowood Press are greatly indebted to our contributors who walked cheerfully all over the county researching the walks for this book. It must be borne in mind that while all the details of these walks (hedges, fences, stiles, and so on) were correct at the time of going to print, the countryside is constantly changing and we cannot be held responsible if details in the walk descriptions are found to be inaccurate. We would be grateful if walkers would let us know of any major alterations to the walks described so that we may incorporate any changes in future editions. Please write to THE 100 WALKS SERIES, The Crowood Press, Crowood House, Ramsbury, Marlborough, Wiltshire SN8 2HE. Walkers are strongly advised to take with them the relevant map for the area and Ordnance Survey maps are recommended for each walk. The walks are organised by dividing the county arbitrarily into four areas – north-east, north-west, south-west and south-east – and are then listed by length – from approximately 3 miles to 12 miles. No attempt has been made to estimate how long the walks will take as this can vary so greatly depending on the strength and fitness of the walkers and the time spent exploring the points of interest highlighted. Nearly all the walks are circular and the majority offer a recommended place to seek refreshments. Telephone numbers of these pubs and cafés are included in case you want to check on opening times, meals available, and so on.

We hope you enjoy exploring the beautiful county of Gloucestershire in the best possible way – on foot – and ask that you cherish its beautiful places by always remembering the country code:

Enjoy the country and respect its life and work
Guard against all risk of fire
Fasten all gates
Keep dogs under close control
Keep to public footpaths across all farmland
Use gates and stiles to cross field boundaries
Leave all livestock, machinery and crops alone
Take your litter home
Help to keep all water clean
Protect wildlife, plants and trees
Make no unnecessary noise

Good walking.

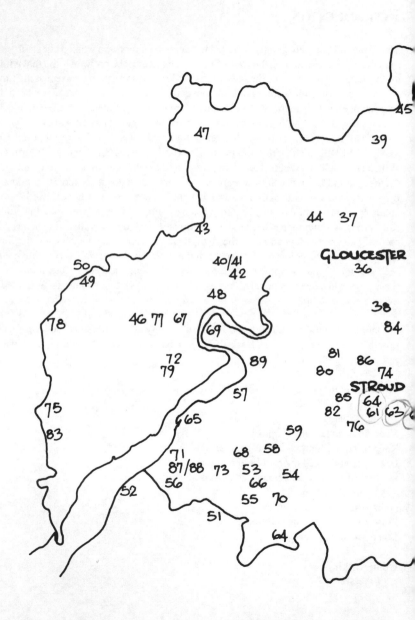

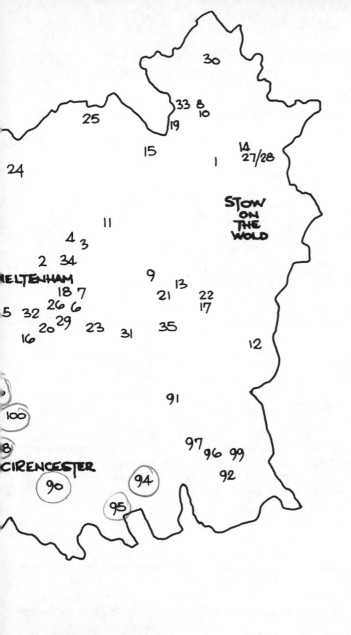

30

33 8
10
25

19

15

24

1

14
27/28

STOW
ON
THE
WOLD

11

4 3

2 34

HELTENHAM

9

18 7

21 13

22

26 6

17

5 32

12

20 29

23

31

35

16

91

100

97

8

96 99

CIRENCESTER

92

90

94

95

Walk 1   BOURTON-ON-THE-HILL AND SEZINCOTE   3m (5km)

Maps: OS Sheets Landranger 151; Pathfinder SP 03/13.

An interesting ramble across fields and parkland.

Start: At 175325, the telephone kiosk in Bourton-on-the-Hill.

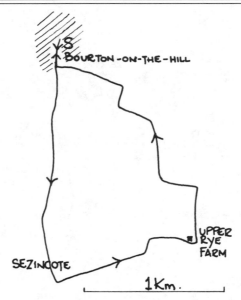

Just 50 yards up the road to the left by some horse boxes is a footpath sign to Sezincote and Longborough. Take the track left 150 yards to a gate and into a field, a further 150 yards with a wall on your right, and pass through another gate. Keep straight ahead, passing through a third gate, and continue now with the hedge on your left.

This hedge turns left by some trees, but keep straight ahead, making for woodland. This is a strip of trees surrounding the parkland. Follow waymarks and pass through two kissing gates. Now, inside the park, start veering right, cross an estate road and go down the slope to the right corner, passing at one point between two trees and a facing fence. You then pass through another strip of woodland through two gates. Carry on straight ahead across the next field. To your left now is a lake (we saw two herons fishing here), and to your right is the magnificent **Sezincote Manor**.

Pass through another gate and go up the field veering right to arrive at a fence in front of woodland. Continue to the far corner and pass through a kissing gate on to a road. Turn left and follow road for about $^1/_2$ mile to Upper Rye Farm. Take the farm track to the right and then go left through a gate following waymarks to pass behind farm, and down road. Go over two cattle grids and by the second, pass over a stile into field on the left.

With hedge left proceed to bottom of field, go over footbridge and turn right following hedge. You then come to a stile giving access to an enclosed path on your right. Carry on through, over another stile into a field and straight on to an estate road. Cross this by two stiles (mind the barbed wire here) and into another field. In 100 yards turn right on to a path between hedges and at the facing hedge (150 yards) turn left. Following hedge right, cross three fields to arrive opposite the church where you turn right and return to Bourton-on-the-Hill.

POINTS OF INTEREST:

Sezincote Manor – Built by Sir Charles Cockerell in 1805 after he had had a spell serving in India. It also influenced the Prince Regent who built the Brighton Pavilion in 1812. The house is open Thursdays and Fridays in the summer 2.30-6.00, while the gardens are open on Thursdays, Fridays and Bank Holiday Mondays from 2.00-6.00. Access to it is down the A44 towards Moreton-in-Marsh from Bourton-on-the-Hill.

Opposite the entrance are the Cotswold Falconry Centre and Batsford Arboretum Garden Centre.

REFRESHMENTS:

The Horse and Groom (tel no: 0386 700413) is on the A44 at the top of Bourton-on-the-Hill.

Walk 2   **GOLD CUP CIRCULAR**   3m (5km)

Maps: OS Sheets Landranger 163; Pathfinder SO 82/92.

An easy, fairly level walk around the perimeter of the racecourse.
Start: At 963257, the racecourse entrance in Southam Lane, Southam, where you may park on non-race days.

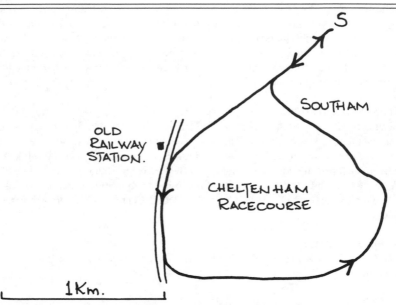

Cross the stile on to **Cheltenham Racecourse** approach and walk towards the course, visible on the higher ground ahead. In about 75 yards leave the tarmac through a gate on your right which leads to a dismantled railway track, and continue towards the over-bridge ahead. Shortly after entering the platform of the now extinct Racecourse Station, fork left up the bank and leave the track behind. Go past the old Ticket Office, through the iron gate and, without crossing the road, straight ahead along the path just visible between the road and the racecourse fencing on your left. After passing the second entrance gate to the course, go over a stile on your left, located at the end of a closely boarded fence, and into the car park. Walk now as close as possible to the racecourse administration buildings on your left with the large car park area on your right, passing a touring caravan site, and on to a firm footpath which skirts the perimeter fence.

Continue with the course on your left, noting the jumps and ignoring tempting side tracks. Shortly, you will come to the first of three iron stiles, each with a unique device to enable your dog to negotiate the obstruction, after which the clear track goes away to some houses on the right. However, you should continue on the minor path, still close to the perimeter fence, and when the course swings sharply away to your left in a long straight in front of the main grandstands, go over the stile ahead, and across a field to another one clearly visible in the far fence. After this stile, steer across the large field towards the top of an overhead sign just discernible towards the right-hand end of a copse, where you will find a final stile. After this turn right on the tarmac lane to return to your car.

N. B. The Gloucester and Warwickshire Railway are hoping to re-open the railway line into Cheltenham at some future time. When that happens, it will still be possible to follow the walk as follows:

Continue along the Racecourse approach, going downhill to cross a stream, then rising again. Go past two stiles on the left then go right (before a left-hand bend) on to a path that leads to a footbridge. Cross, go over a stile and follow the path which runs parallel to the railway track to reach the route as given above near the old Ticket Office.

POINTS OF INTEREST:

Cheltenham Racecourse – Venue of the National Hunt Festival and the Cheltenham Gold Cup Steeplechase, second only in importance 'over the sticks' to the Grand National. The race is held each March, and can be observed without charge from the walk. As a result, on major race days it becomes very crowded, and parking in the vicinity becomes impossible. If you want to see some racing as well as walk, it is best to visit when a minor meeting is being held.

REFRESHMENTS:

Sometimes available on the course, but otherwise in a wide range of eating places in Cheltenham only a mile away.

Walk 3   **WINCHCOMBE AND SUDELEY CASTLE**   3m (5km)
Maps: OS Sheets Landranger 163; Pathfinder SP 02/12.
An easy walk, partly on roads, with views of the castle and town.
Start: At 024285, in the free car park behind the County Library
in Back Lane, Winchcombe.

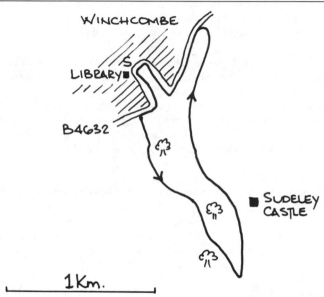

Walk into Cowl Lane, turning right towards the town. At the junction turn right on the
raised pavement and first left into Vineyard Street. Cross the River Isbourne, following
the lane as it bears right and continue for about $^3/_4$ mile, looking for the fine view of
Sudeley Castle on your left. Where the road turns sharply right and slightly uphill, turn
left on a footpath across open grass. Within a few yards cross a wooden footbridge, a
stile, and another wooden bridge, and go up the bank ahead. The path is indistinct at
this point, so steer a course first towards two large trees directly ahead, and then to the
corner of the field near the castle which is close to your right. Go through the kissing
gate, and follow the wide track for a few yards, looking for a wooden gate in the right-
hand fence providing access to a children's activity playground (provided for paying
visitors to the castle).

Follow the footpath diagonally across this playground, over a stile, and continue in the same direction across two large fields until the footpath joins a metalled road. Cross the road at once, and turn left and then right up the narrow alley at the end of the row of cottages. Go through the gate, following the footpath gradually converging on the River Isbourne over three fields and on to a main road. Here, turn left, keeping on the narrow footpath into the town centre. Turn right into North Street by the side of the unique Police Uniforms Museum with a five-hole set of stocks outside, then take the first left into Back Lane to the County Library and the car park.

POINTS OF INTEREST:
Sudeley Castle – A very historic site, visited at various times by Henry VIII and Elizabeth I, and where Henry's sixth wife, Catherine Parr, is buried. Open to the public from April to October. Various and frequent entertainments and exhibitions.
Winchcombe – An ancient town, once the capital of Mercia, and the site of a very important Abbey. Much of historical and architectural interest to be found. The Tourist Information Office is in the town centre, by the stocks. A fascinating Railway Museum will be found in Gloucester Street just beyond the church.

REFRESHMENTS:
Sudeley Castle Restaurant (tel no: 0242 604357). Excellent facilities.
The White Hart (tel no: 0242 603047) and *The Plaisterers* Arms (tel no: 0242 602358) in the main street.
Lady Jane's Tea Rooms (tel no: 0242 603578) is also in the main street and welcomes walkers.
Wesley House Restaurant (tel no: 0242 602366). A high-class venue providing superb meals.

Walk 4   WINCHCOMBE AND LANGLEY HILL $4\frac{1}{2}$m (7km)

Maps: OS Sheets Landranger 163; Pathfinder SP 02/12 and SO 03/13.

A walk over rough hill pasture with fine views.

Start: At 024285, in the free car park behind the County Library in Back Lane, Winchcombe.

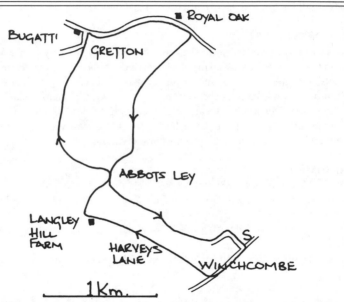

Regain Back Lane, turn left, bear right at the Y-junction into Langley Road and first right into Harvey's Lane. Cross two cattle grids, go through Langley Hill Farm yard and, immediately after passing the last farm building on the left, turn right through a gap in the fence, across the field and through a gate in the far wall. Follow the middle track ahead until you face a dry-stone wall with a cross track running alongside it. The views on your right include Winchcombe (see Walk 3), Stanway Hill, Salter's Hill and Cleeve. Turn left, ignore the blue metal gate on your right, and follow a way marked with a yellow 'W' – the Wychavon Way. Where the track winds temptingly away to the left keep straight ahead to pass over a stile and descend, following the waymarks, over two stiles and some precarious wooden steps, keeping to the right-hand side of the

20

field in which you find yourself. At the bottom right-hand corner cross a stile, bear half-left to the far corner over a stile and follow the small rivulet to a footpath at the rear of the house in front of you. Emerge into Duglinch Lane, Gretton, turn right and at the main street you may seek refreshment by turning left to the Bugatti Inn, just a few yards away, or by turning right through the village to the Royal Oak. Both are good places to eat.

Continue the walk through the village, noting for interest the church and the antique cabinet makers next to the post office. About 100 yards past the Royal Oak turn right and ascend a track signposted 'Gretton Hill', until you reach the blue metal gate mentioned earlier. Turn left, keep the wall on your left, ignoring two wide tracks going off to the right, until you emerge into an open field, which you should cross diagonally to the far corner where there is a stile. For a few yards the footpath is clear, but then steer a course downhill straight towards the tower of Winchcombe Church, through a farm gate to the bottom left-hand corner of the next field. Cross a stile and two others in quick succession, go through two fields, over a final stile and into a bungalow estate. This is Orchard Road, from which you turn first right into Barnmeadow Road. At the end of you will see the library car park again.

REFRESHMENTS:
The Bugatti Inn, Gretton (tel no: 0242 602471). Haunt of motor hill climb enthusiasts attending at nearby Prescott.
The Royal Oak, Gretton (tel no: 0242 602447).

Walk 5 LECKHAMPTON AND THE DEVIL'S CHIMNEY 5m (8km)

Maps: OS Sheets Landranger 163; Pathfinder SO 81/91.

A walk with spectacular views, involving one steep descent.

Start: At 942195, the car park opposite St Peter's Church, Leckhampton.

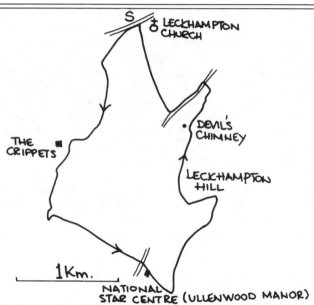

From the car park turn right and just after the farm buildings on the right turn left on to the marked footpath on your left. Keep to the right-hand fence and enter the field by the stile, making for a barely discernible footbridge and stile in the far fence. In the next field pass through a wicket gate in the far fence, continuing along the narrowing meadow to negotiate a stile and footbridge at its apex to reach Crippetts Lane. Turn left and follow the lane which presently passes through ornamental drive gates and then goes gently upwards along an avenue of sweet chestnut trees, passing the entrance to Crippetts Farm on the right. When **The Crippetts** comes into view, turn left on to the marked bridle path and follow it. Just before a metal farm gate it goes sharply right uphill to pass through a gate and then wind through parkland scenery, its clear route marked with specimen conifers planted at intervals on each side of the track.

22

After the next gate, the track joins Greenway Lane: bear left to follow it past the remains of a war-time hospital to a crossroads. Here, go straight over towards Ullenwood, as signposted, and immediately after the entrance on your right to The National Star Centre, go left on a waymarked bridle path to Leckhampton Hill. This is part of the Cotswold Way. When the track forms a T-junction with a metalled lane, go left, downhill, for about 200 yards to enter a waymarked footpath on the right which rises up along the edge of a quarry/car park to reach the escarpment of Leckhampton Hill. Continue with the panoramic views on your left and a dry-stone wall on your right until the wall ends, and the distinct track swings away to the right. Here, fork left to go downhill along the edge of the hill, within a few yards passing The Devil's Chimney, a prominent rock formation on your left, and noting far below the spire of St Peter's Church, Leckhampton, from where you started the walk. Follow the shingle track along the edge of the hill, and (with great care) as it descends very steeply to a small open area where there are abandoned quarry buildings and a concrete milestone set at a junction of ways. Go sharp left in the direction of the arrow on the milestone, and within six or seven yards bear right, downhill, between trees and bushes on a pleasant footpath which gradually becomes a wide metalled drive.

Upon reaching the main road, turn left, uphill, ignoring the first signed footpath to Leckhampton, passing the lay-by on the left to the concealed second fingerpost (to Leckhampton Church) opposite a house named Leckhampton Grange. Turn right, over the stile, and into the field. The path here is indistinct, so follow the fingerposts downhill through scrubby woodland into an open field, then steer slightly to the left of Leckhampton Church. Pass through a gap in the first hedge, to a stile located between two mature oak trees in the bottom right-hand corner of the next field. Bear right to a stile and cross a meadow, making for the corner where it joins the churchyard and Church Road. After the final stile turn right and back to the start.

POINTS OF INTEREST:

The Crippetts – One-time home of Dr. Edward Wilson, who perished with Scott on the Antarctic expedition of 1912, and where much of the planning was done.

The Devil's Chimney – A stony outcrop about which there is much dispute – a natural phenomenon or a quarryman's prank?

St Peter's Church, Leckhampton – Medieval with a 14th century tower and spire.

REFRESHMENTS:

The Malvern Inn, Leckhampton Road, Cheltenham (tel no: 0242 526763).

Walk 6   KILKENNY TO FOXCOTE   5m (8km)

Maps: OS Sheets Landranger 163; Pathfinder SP 01/11.

A fine ramble over the hills with wonderful scenery.

Start: At 004185, the car park at Kilkenny picnic area.

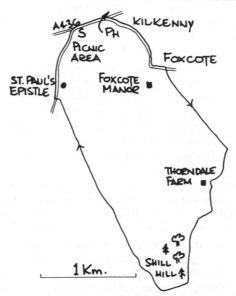

Leave the car park, noting **St Paul's Epistle** the mound behind the picnic area and walk down to the A436. Turn right to the Kilkenny Arms and take the Foxcote road to the right. Follow this road to the bottom of the hill, passing in front of the Manor gates and by a disused chapel, turn left. Where the road ends look for a stile on your right and cross it to enter a field. Follow the hedge on your left ascending the field to a gate and then going slightly left, make for a strip of trees at the top. A gate on your left gives access to a track between walls leading to a road. Turn right to Thorndale Farm, following the road below the farm buildings to a field gate below the farmhouse. Pass through into the field and continue along the track. At the next gate do not pass through but turn right to ascend to a wood.

    Enter the wood by a gate and follow a good path up the lower wood edge, with a wall on the left. After about $^1/_2$ mile, at the top of the rise, turn right across a track and enter a field with a hedge on the left. Climb to the top and at the next gate pass through and turn right following the hedge on the right. Straight ahead is another gate, pass through and climb the bank with a wall on the right.

At the next gate, keep straight ahead with the wall now on the left and with views down the **Foxcote Valley**. Stay with the same wall and pass through another gate. Do not descend towards Foxcote: Ahead lies a small compound – the path goes through it – and beyond is a stile. Go over and turn left, 50 yards to the road. Turn right and the car park start is about $^{1}/_{2}$ mile further on.

POINTS OF INTEREST:

St Paul's Epistle – This is where a local parish priest, walking the parish bounds with his parishioners, paused to read from the Bible. Deer are seen quite regularly in this area.

Foxcote Valley – There are very good views in all directions when on this walk – towards the Shiptons and Withington on the outward part, and towards Hilcot and then Cheltenham on the return.

REFRESHMENTS:

The Kilkenny Arms (tel no: 0242 820341).

Walk 7   SYREFORD AND SEVENHAMPTON   5m (8km)

Maps: OS Sheets Landranger 163; Pathfinder SP 02/12.

A lovely walk near the source of the River Coln.

Start: At 029204, Syreford Farm, just off the A436 near its junction with the A40.

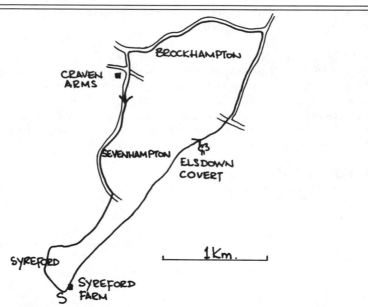

Take the bridleway opposite the farm, noting first the old **Railway**, and climb steadily north-east. There are good views from here down into the valley of the **River Coln.** Pass Elsdown Covert on your right and 1$^1/_2$ miles from the start you will come to the Brockhampton road. Continue straight over on to a minor road – no signpost – with a wood on the left. After a mile turn left at a signpost which reads 'Brockhampton 1$^3/_4$ miles'.

As you descend the views open up and are particularly good to the north. At **Brockhampton** the road bends left past the school. Follow it to the crossroads and go straight over. If you are in need of rest there is a seat here, and the Craven Arms is to the right.

Continue on the minor road for $^1/_2$ mile to **Sevenhampton.** Once again a seat is handy by the ford, and a path over the stream goes up to the church if you would like to visit it. Continuing straight ahead, the walk goes down the valley. The road finishes at some farm buildings, but a track continues through a white gate. The track runs between walls to a field gate. Pass through into the field and turn right, following the wall to your right. Go down to a metal gate and pass through and then go straight ahead to enter the wood facing you through a wicket gate. Continue through the wood and, on emerging, take a rough track by some cottages going slightly left down to the road at **Syreford.** Turn left and walk up the slope to the start.

POINTS OF INTEREST:
The Railway – This is the old line which once ran from Cheltenham to the north Cotswolds.
River Coln – Rises just north of Brockhampton at Charlton Abbots and runs 25 miles to join the Thames at Lechlade.
Brockhampton – There was once a fine deer park here belonging to Brockhampton House, seen over the valley as you descend to the village.
Sevenhampton – With its ford in the bottom and church on the opposite bank, this is a village in two parts divided by the Coln.
Syreford – A fine Roman statuette of Mars was found here.

REFRESHMENTS:
Craven Arms, Brockhampton (tel no: 0793 820410)

Walk 8   CHIPPING CAMPDEN AND DOVER'S HILL   5m (8km)
Maps: OS Sheets Landranger 151; Pathfinder SP 03/13 and SP 04/14.
An interesting walk in and around Campden.
Start: St James' Church, Chipping Campden

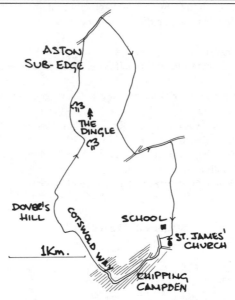

St James' Church in **Chipping Campden** is also the start of the Cotswold Way. Go down Church Street and left into High Street. Walk down to Lower High Street and turn right by St Catherine's church, signposted 'Back Ends and Hoo Lane'. Hoo Lane (the Cotswold Way) is on the left and you follow this lane up to a bridleway and on up to the road.

Turn left and after a few yards look for the sign right to **Dover's Hill**. Follow the hedge and continue to a stile. Cross over and on to Dover's Hill. Turn right: this is your general direction north-east across two fields to a road. Cross this and enter the wood through a gate, turning left down the slope. This is The Dingle. Go down about 400 yards to a field gate, pass through and go down the field with a wood on the right to the white gate at the bottom. Pass through and go over a stile on the left a few yards further

28

on. Follow the hedge and stream on the left down across two fields and go over the stile by a wooded area at the bottom and join the road. Turn right.

Follow the road for 400 yards up the slope and, at the top, turn right on to a bridleway. With the hedge on the left cross two fields to the top of the rise. Go over the stile and, bearing right, pass to the left of facing trees, and go on down over a track to arrive at a gate in the far corner. Proceed up the slope ahead, following the waymarks, through a gate and between two stone pillars to the copse at the top. Go through the gate and follow the track which merges with a metalled road, passing a farmhouse to the main road.

Cross over on to the Hidcote Boyce road and continue ahead for approximately 500 yards to a footpath on the right. Go over the stile with a hedge on the left and go down the field to a facing hedge. Cross the stream by a footbridge. Turn right and follow the edge of the field to farm buildings. Continue ahead towards the school buildings, but keep left of a ditch and playing fields down to the bottom of the field. Here turn right by the school buildings and round to a road. Turn left and go down to the start of the walk.

POINTS OF INTEREST:
Dover's Hill – This is the venue for the Cotswold 'Olympic' Games in late May, a revival of the games introduced by Robert Dover in the 17th century. There are fine views across the Vale of Evesham.
Chipping Campden – St James' Church is one of the tallest Cotswold churches with 12 pinnacles on the tower. Next down Church Street are the almshouses on the right built in the shape of the letter I. Opposite is the cart and coach water dip where wooden wheels were wetted to stop shrinkage. In the High Street is the old Woolstaplers' Hall on the left, with the Market Hall further down. Nearly every house in this street carries the mark of the Cotswold stonemason.

REFRESHMENTS:
Numerous in Chipping Campden.

Walk 9   GUITING WOOD AND GUITING POWER   5m (8km)

Maps: OS Sheets Landranger 163; Pathfinder SP 02/12.

An easy walk, fairly level through woods and farmland.

Start: At 084258, the signed car park near Kineton.

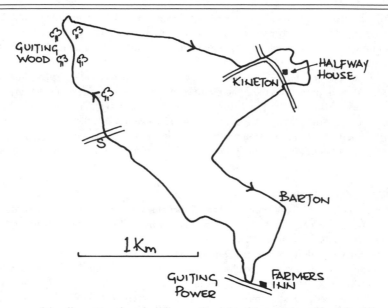

The car park is adjacent to a farm building on the right of the gated road from Roel Farm to Kineton, about 100 yards beyond the first gate. Turn right out of the car park, over the road on which you arrived and follow the wide track across parkland, through a farm gate by a lodge and **Guiting Wood,** until you arrive at a T-junction. Turn right and continue straight ahead, over a cross-track, for almost 1 mile to a metalled road, where you turn left into **Kineton**. At the staggered crossroads, go down the hill marked for 'Ford', unless you need refreshments, in which case, continue on the level to the Halfway House just a few yards away.

At the bottom of the hill cross the footbridge, turning right and right again to follow the course of the River Windrush, crossing it again by another footbridge and going up hill to a T-junction. Turn left and almost at once go right, through a farm gate, keeping to the left of farm buildings. Follow a footpath straight ahead across three fields towards Castlett Farm, keeping close to the hedge or wall on your left. At the end of the third field cross a waymarked stile. Go straight ahead down steps and a drive giving access to a house on your left, to a lane. Go left for about $^1/_2$ mile, and just as the lane starts to descend turn right at a footpath marker crossing a field by a well-defined track towards Guiting Power. After the next stile, descend to and cross the stream, then go up the opposite bank to another stile giving access to a lane leading to the village green. Turn right. Sources of refreshment are available in the village, from where you turn first right beyond the Post Office into a lane which, on the edge of the village, becomes a track descending through scrub and woodland. At the fork bear left up the bank then turn right just opposite farm buildings on to a good track through open fields which takes you back to the start.

PLACES OF INTEREST:
Guiting Wood – A thumping noise on the right half-way through the wood is a hydraulic ram, a kind of water pump quite common in this area.
Kineton – An attractive village, with old Cotswold cottages near fords.

REFRESHMENTS:
The Halfway House, Kineton (tel no: 04515 344).
Ye Old Inn, Guiting Power (tel no: 04515 392).
The Farmers Arms, Guiting Power (tel no: 04515 358).

Walk 10 **Dover's Hill and Broad Campden** 5m (8km)

Maps: OS Sheets Landranger 151; Pathfinder SP 03/13.

A walk which goes through two lovely north Cotswold villages.

Start: At 137396, the National Trust car park on Dover's Hill.

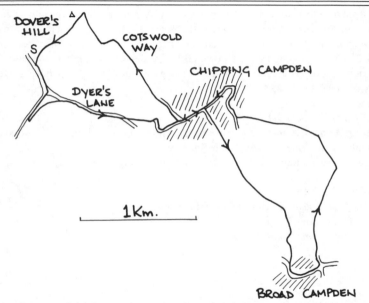

Leave the car park back on to the road, and turn left down to the crossroads. Turn right to see the **Kiftsgate Stone** to the right, in the wood. Retrace your steps along the road to the seat on the right and go half-right across a field towards Chipping Campden. Go down to Dyer's Lane, and turn right. Go down to a thatched house on right. Opposite here, on the left, is a footpath to Chipping Campden (see Walk 8). Take this, enter a field and follow round to the right to the far side. Go between houses to the road – Littleworth – turn right and descend to the main road. Turn left up Chipping Campden's main street and at the Post Office turn right through an archway and go through the yard of the Noel Arms Inn. At the bottom go straight ahead up George Lane to pass school playing fields on the right. Where the footpath meets a road, turn left on to a footpath which runs parallel to the road with a hedge, and is followed to **Broad Campden**.

At the point where the road bends right, continue ahead up a bank. After nearly

200 yards take the right track at a fork and follow the wall on the left down to Broad Campden. Pass through a wicket gate and follow a fence round to the right to the start of an avenue of lime trees. Follow the footpath and turn left through wicket gate to pass down an alley to the Quaker Meeting House (1663). Turn right and go along the road in front of a row of charming cottages down to the crossroads by St Michael's Church. The Baker's Arms is just up round the corner to the right here, and there is a conveniently placed seat in front of the church. To see the village, continue ahead on the road and follow it right round. You will see from the map that the road forms a circle around the village: walk anti-clockwise to arrive at Hayes Lodge by a letterbox, and turn left down a road marked 'Unsuitable for Motors'.

After 100 yards go through a gate on the right, beside a house named 'Hollybush'. After 100 yards go through a second gate, and after a further 100 yards through a third. Follow the hedge, left, descending 150 yards to a stile, right, and over it into an orchard. Follow the hedge and fence left along the bottom of the field and go left over stiles and a footbridge into a field. Turn right, following the stream and at the far end go through a gap in the hedge and cross to a facing hedge and another gap. Keeping parallel with the top hedge, cross this cultivated field to a stile in the facing fence, in line with some tall trees ahead. Go over and, passing between trees in the field, make for the far right corner. Go over a stile and right towards trees, following the River Cam. You will pass a stone arch on the right: 100 yards ahead go through a gate on the right at the start of a solid wooden fence. Follow the path round, over a stile and on to a rough road. Go up to Calf Lane and turn right. When you reach Church Street turn left and go into High Street. St James' Church, the start of the Cotswold Way, is to your right.

Walk straight down the main street as far as St Catherine's Church to your right in Lower High Street. Turn right towards Back Ends and Hoo Lane. This is the Cotswold Way (waymarked with a white spot on top of yellow or blue waymarks) and will be followed back to **Dover's Hill** (see Walk 8). Follow Hoo Lane and a bridleway to Kingcombe Lane at the top of the hill. Turn left and in 50 yards turn right to walk up a field, over a stile and on to Dover's Hill. Turn left for the car park.

POINTS OF INTEREST:

Broad Campden – Both Chipping Campden and Broad Campden are a photographer's paradise, though they are quite different; the former using the local stone for the complete buildings while the latter has many thatched roofs.

The Kiftsgate Stone – This is a moot point. It was certainly used as a meeting place for the Kiftsgate Hundred in Saxon times. The Magna Carta was read from here and kings were proclaimed from it.

Walk 11   STUMPS CROSS AND HAILES   5¼m (9km)

Maps: OS Sheets Landranger 150; Pathfinder SP 02/12 and SP 03/13.

A varied walk with good views, visiting the ruins of Hailes Abbey.
Start: At 076304, Stumps Cross at the top of Stanway Hill on the B4077.

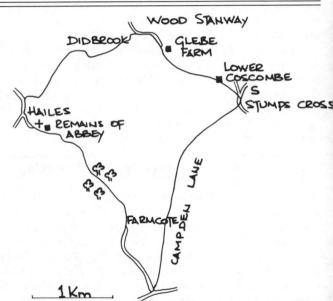

Go through the gate opposite the lane at the top of the hill (be careful if you have to cross the busy main road) to reach a wide track with a fine line of trees on the right. Continue on this ancient way, Campden Lane, noting the bizarre combination of old and new on the right where a very dilapidated metal barn is supported on staddle stones. Pass through two fields, a wide strip of scrubby land, then through a gate and between overgrown hedgerows for about 1 mile until you meet a metalled lane at a junction. Turn right towards Farmcote – note the old village pump opposite the first farmhouse in the village – and, after passing the large house on the left just beyond St Faith's church, bear left to pass in front of farm cottages on a descending bridle path. It is said that Henry VIII's chief minister Thomas Cromwell sat in the fields on the right, in 1539,

34

to watch the destruction of Hailes Abbey below. The track passes through woodland and orchards and, when the surface becomes metalled road again, you will see the ruins of **Hailes Abbey** on your left and **Hailes Parish Church** on your right. Both are well worth a visit, especially the latter.

Continue along the road to a T-junction where you turn right, and in a few yards, where the road bends away to the left, go through a gate in the right-hand hedge and follow a waymarked track across fields. When the track peters out and becomes a less distinct footpath, a line of venerable oak trees help to identify the route. The village of Didbrook is visible on the left, but keep straight on to enter Wood Stanway. Turn left at the first T-junction and right at the second to walk through the hamlet to Glebe Farm where the metalled lane ends. Walk through the farmyard and follow the track indicated by the footpath sign to Stumps Cross. This route goes through open fields, in a generally uphill direction, and is clearly marked as the Cotswold Way (yellow arrows accompanied by a white dot). In case of doubt keep the line of power cables on your right until you reach Lower Coscombe. Do not pass through the farm buildings as the former Right of Way has been extinguished. Instead, turn right to follow the waymarks across fields, climbing steadily towards a line of trees on the crest of the hill. When you reach the trees turn left to follow the wall back to the starting point at Stumps Cross.

POINTS OF INTEREST:

Hailes Abbey – Ruins of a Cistercian Abbey founded in 1246. Once one of the richest and most powerful abbeys in England, largely through its acquisition of a precious relic, a phial of the Holy Blood of Christ, which was later deemed to be fraudulent by Henry VIII who ordered the destruction of the abbey in 1539.

Hailes Parish Church – 12th-century, with a timbered bell-cote, medieval wall paintings and much more of interest.

REFRESHMENTS:

The Plough Inn, Ford (tel no: 038673 215).
The Pheasant Inn, Toddington (tel no: 024269 271).

Walk 12   SHERBORNE AND THE BARRINGTONS   6m (9.5km)

Maps: OS Sheets Landranger 163; Pathfinder SP 01/11 & 21/31.
A varied walk through delightful villages and over farmland.
Start: At 173145, the Post Office in Sherborne.

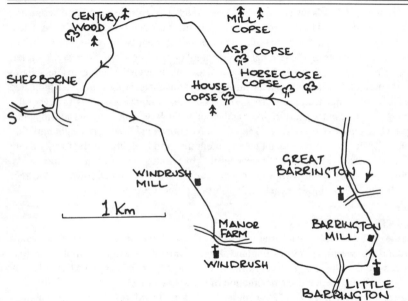

Walk east to a T-junction. Turn left and shortly go right between cottages. Cross two waymarked stiles, go across a field, through a gate, and follow the path along the right-hand hedges. Keep the power cables on your right until you reach the corner of a third field, go through a gap under the cables and follow a distinct path across the next field to the corner of another field. Follow the hedge, right, going over a stile and passing a stone barn, right. At this point you can see the River Windrush on your left. Go through the gate at the right of the barn, cross the lane and up the steps ahead to a stile. Keep left until you meet the far wall, where you turn right and over a stone stile into a wide track leading into Windrush village.

Turn left at the telephone kiosk to pass **St Peter's Church**, Windrush, on your right. About 100 yards beyond the church go through a kissing gate on the right into a field. The path bears half-left, skirting the corner of a garden, then heads towards two

36

ancient trees, to pass through the right-hand of two farm gates. Keep to the left of the field, going over a stone stile, and on to a wooden stile by a large water trough. Ahead you can see Little Barrington, and by steering slightly to the right of the church you will come to a wooden double stile, after which a wide track leads to a stile in the wall ahead. Cross a field, go between farm buildings and across the farmyard to a lane. Go right, then left at the pump, to go left of the green, and just beyond the Post Office go right, crossing the green to enter the 'No Through Road'. This soon becomes a footpath, but in about 200 yards reverts once more to a metalled road which will lead you to St Peter's Church. If you are not visiting the church, turn left to cross the Windrush by footbridge, going along a footpath that passes Barrington Mill to reach **Great Barrington**.

From the War Memorial take the road towards Great Rissington for about 300 yards, keeping the Deer Park wall on your left, and then turn left into the 'No Through Road' for Manor Farm. Do not enter the farm, but turn right along a track skirting it and passing between two woods, House Copse, left, and Horseclose Copse, right. Cross a stone bridge over a stream and bear slightly left to reach a track, with a fence on its right, passing through open fields. The track runs parallel with the lower edge of, first, Asp Copse and then Mill Copse on your right, but when you reach the far side of the latter turn sharp left downhill following the track as it winds through scrub woodland to cross over the River Windrush again. There are wild deer in this area and you will probably see deer slots in the mud. The track now improves but where it enters Century Wood, turn left through a gap to follow the edge of the wood to a farm gate in the fence ahead. Here, go half-right to the far corner of the field, cross the Sherborne Brook, and turn right on to a track which, after skirting a small sewage farm enclosure, becomes a concrete road. On the edge of **Sherborne** turn left through a farm gate and then right over the stile, on to the path by which you started the walk, and back to the start.

PLACES OF INTEREST:

St Peter's Church, Windrush – Norman. Has a famous doorway with beakheads.
St Peter's Church, Little Barrington – Norman church with original sculptured tympanum built into the north wall.
Great Barrington – One-time home of Thomas Strong, chief mason of St Paul's Cathedral. Barrington Park has deer herds. The church of St Mary contains a fine memorial to two small children of the Bray family who died in the Great Plague.
Sherborne – A delightful village with a 14th-century church.

REFRESHMENTS:

The Fox Inn, Great Barrington (tel no: 04514 385) Local ales.

Walk 13   NAUNTON AND GUITING POWER   6m (9.5km)

Maps: OS Sheets Landranger 163; Pathfinder SP 02/12.
An interesting and varied walk to the north-west of Naunton.
Start: The Black Horse in Naunton.

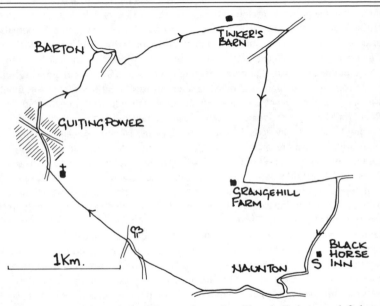

Walk west on the road through the village as far as the village hall, then turn left down the road opposite the hall to reach the River Windrush. Pass through a gate, turn right and proceed to the next gate, go through and on to the road. You will have passed an interesting dovecote on your right.

Proceed to the main road and turn left uphill. After 400 yards look for a stile on the right, about 100 yards past the Naunton road sign. If you miss the stile use the gate just a little further on. Cross the field to a stile and then make a line for a copse slightly left. Pass through a gateway, with the copse on your left, and proceed to the road. Turn right down to a T-junction. Straight opposite is an entry into a field. Go through and take the path, making for the facing hedge. Go through a gate and into a conservation area – note the lake on the left. Go down the bank through a gate and straight across the field. Make a line for the church: there is a stile in a wall a few yards from the left corner

38

of the field. Pass over the stile into a field beside St Michael's Church and go on to another stile and gate and on to a road. Continue ahead passing the hall and school to the war memorial in **Guiting Power**. The Farmer's Inn is to the right here.

Cross over to a 'No Through Road' and proceed ahead on to a track to a gate. Cross the stile beside the gate and follow the path down to a stream at the bottom. Cross a stile and go up the bank. Now do not cross the stile ahead but go over the one on the right marked for Barton. In the field follow the hedge left,and where the hedge turns go straight across to the facing hedge. Cross the stile and two more beside Little Windrush Farm to reach a road in Barton village. Follow the road down to the main road, turn right and go over the river bridge.

At the far side of the bridge, turn left through a gate on to a track. After 100 yards it bends right to another gate. Pass through and immediately turn left following the hedge on the left up a bank. Follow this track for 1 mile past Tinker's Barn where you might see some of the animals from the **Cotswold Farm Park**. At the track's end turn right on a road and after nearly 400 yards turn left along a definite track with a hedge on the right. Follow this track for $^1/_2$ mile to another road. Turn left along the ridge road for $^1/_2$ mile, then turn right down to **Naunton** and the start of the walk.

POINTS OF INTEREST:
Cotswold Farm Park – The most comprehensive collection of rare farm animal breeds in Britain.
Guiting Power – A typical Cotswold village.
Naunton – A fine small town. Especially noteworthy are the 17th-century dovecote, the Baptist chapel and the church.

REFRESHMENTS:
The Farmer's Inn, Guiting Power (tel no: 04515 358).
The Black Horse Inn, Naunton (tel no: 04515 378).

Maps: OS Sheets Landranger 151; Pathfinder SP 03/13.
A walk in the countryside surrounding Blockley.
Start: Anywhere in Blockley – it is especially convenient close to
the Lower Brook Hotel.

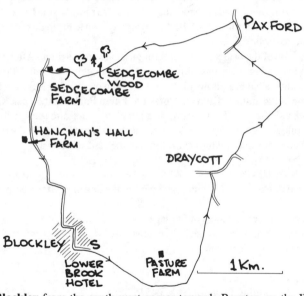

Leave **Blockley** from the south-west corner towards Bourton-on-the-Water. A few
yards past the Lower Brook Hotel take the farm road to Pasture Farm on the left. Follow
this over a cattle grid and start to climb. Where the track turns left follow the path
waymarked to the right of a barn. Continue uphill, following a hedge on the right to the
beech trees at the top. Turn left, pass through a wicket gate and on to the corner of a field.
Pass through a gate on the right and then through another gate to the left a few yards
further on. Cross the field, aiming right of some trees, and go down a bank, following
the fence on the left to pass through a gate. Descend to the bottom of the field after
negotiating a high stile. Go down to the house at the bottom and pass to the right by a
stream. Go on to the drive, out to a road and on down to Draycott village.

   Turn right at the crossroads on to the Aston Magna road. Where the road bends right take the bridleway through a gate to the left. Continue ahead to a railway bridge and pass under. In 100 yards turn left towards a farm and cross the field. Go over a bridge, up a bank and keep left on the track to reach a road. Turn right up into Paxford.

Go up round to the left to the first cottages and take the bridleway, left, by a letterbox. Go between farm buildings and round to the left through a gate into a field. Continue ahead to the railway, cross the line by using the wicket gates and proceed forward on the same path through several gates to a road with a hedge and stream on the left. Cross the road to a stile slightly left and enter the Northwick Business Centre. Continue ahead up the road with buildings on the left and Sedgecombe Wood on the right. Go to the top right corner of the wood and through a gate on the right to a concrete road to Sedgecombe Farm. Within 20 yards of the road take a path – not very distinct – to the left through trees and continue ahead to a gate leading to the road on the right. You can go straight up the Sedgecombe Farm road and turn left on the road if you wish.

Proceed along the road towards Blockley, past Hangman's Hall Farm, and as the road descends look for a bridleway right. Go up a bank into a field, turn left and through two gates into another field. Go down the bank, through a gate and up the opposite side. At the top you will see a soccer pitch; go to the left and over a stile and across to the road. Turn right and walk down into Blockley.

POINTS OF INTEREST:

Blockley – Full of interest with many old buildings. The least spoilt of Cotswold villages. A feature of many of the houses is a wrought-iron porch. The Church of St. Peter and St Paul, Norman with 17th and 18th-century towers, is worth a visit but our favourite building is the converted mill at the bottom of the village.

REFRESHMENTS:
Many places available in Blockley.

Walk 15   STANTON TO STANWAY   6m (9.5km)

Maps: OS Sheets Landranger 150; Pathfinder SP 03/13.

A walk through woodland and park, visiting two renowned Cotswold villages and the site of an ancient settlement.

Start: At 068343, the car park at Stanton village.

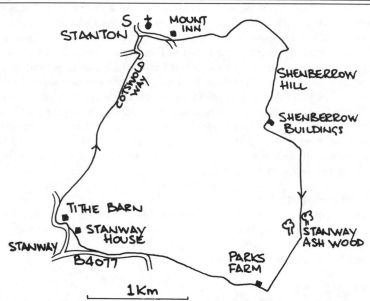

Turn right out of the car park and through the village of **Stanton**, ignoring the road to Stanway. Note the age of the houses on the right and the beautiful colour of the stone of which they are built. On the left by a Cross you will see the way to St Michael's Church if you care to make the short diversion. Take the left fork and ascend, going to the right of The Mount Inn where good food and local ale may be obtained. Loop around the back of the inn to a footpath going off to the right. Pass through a farm gate and keep on the main track uphill, through an open field, another gate and along a fenced track. Be sure to stop occasionally to catch your breath and admire the fine views behind you. At the top of the hill, about 30 yards beyond a narrow wood on your right, turn right on to the Cotswold Way (waymarked with an arrow and a white dot), and follow the wide track until you approach Shenberrow Buildings, a farm overlooking the site of an ancient settlement. If you wish to visit the **Shenberrow** earthworks, continue past the farm and turn right to the edge of the escarpment. Otherwise, turn left before the farm on a bridleway which passes behind a small copse and through the farm buildings.

Directly behind the farm the bridleway turns left, in a south-easterly direction, and if you look to your left you will see, on the horizon, Broadway Tower, a folly from which eight counties can be viewed. When you meet a cross-track, turn right and then walk in a straight line, passing through three farm gates, and merging with a broader track coming in from your right. The track passes through a narrow belt of trees, known as Stanway Ash Plantation, to a T-junction with an unfenced lane. Turn sharp right and walk alongside the plantation for about $\frac{1}{3}$ mile, and at the first crossroads turn right on to an unmetalled track. Pass a farm building on the right and descend through woodland, ignoring all side tracks, to pass by a few cottages and join the B4077. Walk on the right-hand side of the road for about 400 yards, then go over a stile in the right-hand hedge where there is a finger post to Stanway, and bear left to follow the footpath around the corner of a wall, passing a timber yard on the left, to join the metalled road in **Stanway**. Turn right and follow the road, passing on the right the ornate gateway to Stanway House (attributed by some to Inigo Jones), the church, the fine tithe barn and on the left the village cricket pavilion mounted upon staddle stones. Many famous cricketers have displayed their talents here. Directly opposite the cricket pavilion go over a stile on your right to follow the very adequate Cotswold Way signs through parkland to Stanton. Turn right when you enter the village, and first left back to the car park.

PLACES OF INTEREST:
Stanton – Perhaps the Cotswolds' most beautiful village. St Peter's Church is Norman.
Shenberrow – An Iron Age hill fort with double rampart and ditch defences enclosing 3 acres.
Stanway – Composed of lovely ancient stone buildings. Full of history. The House was built by the Tracy family: William de Tracy was one of the four knights who murdered Thomas a Becket. Later the house was owned by Dr Robert Dover who rescued Alexander Selkirk, the original Robinson Crusoe, from his desert island.

REFRESHMENTS:
The Mount Inn, Stanway (tel no: 038673 316).

Walk 16   CRICKLEY HILL AND COBERLEY $6\frac{1}{2}$m (10km)
Maps: OS Sheets Landranger 163; Pathfinder SO 81/91.
A walk with everything – views, hills and valleys.
Start: At 927163, the car park at the Crickley Hill Country Park.

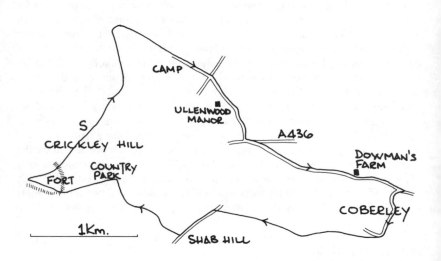

From the car park walk north-west following the Cotswold Way (the yellow arrows
with dot). Go up the steps out of the car park, through a kissing gate into a field. Follow
a path between beech trees gradually turning north towards some fir trees. Proceed on
the left of this wood along a bank with fine views towards Gloucester. Pass over stiles
to reach a road and turn right towards Ullenwood. You will reach a crossroads in about
$\frac{1}{2}$ mile: go straight over towards Ullenwood Star Centre. Continuing ahead you will
pass the Centre where the Cotswold Way goes left. Ignore this and continue ahead to
pass a small lake on the right and a golf clubhouse on the left. Walk on to reach the main
road, the A436. Turn left and in about 200 yards take the right turning for Coberley.

In about 1 mile as you reach Coberley, passing Dowman's Farm, take the road
sharp right. In $\frac{1}{4}$ mile you reach the Cowley road: turn right and almost immediately
left on to a track by a few ash trees. Go through a gate and continue uphill with the

'outside pig unit' on the right. Ignore the gateway to the left after 300 yards and proceed uphill. Go through two more gateways and across to a farm set in a copse. Go forward again to a wood in front of you where you turn left. At the end of the wood there is a field to the right and your path, also right, lies at the far end of this field. With a hedge on your left proceed to a stile, go over and on to two more stiles on either side of a green track. Still heading in the same direction go down to a stile at the corner of a wood. Go over this and through the wood down to the main road by the Air Balloon pub. Turn right. Follow the wall of the public house down to a crossroads and at the far end, near some cottages, cross the A417. There is a bridleway on the right: follow it through a gate and into a field. Now follow the Cotswold Way markers again and you will go left to the south-west end of **Crickley Hill** and then return to the start of the walk.

POINTS OF INTEREST:
Coberley – Dick Whittington once lived here – his parents are buried in the churchyard at the far end of the village. There is a heart burial monument here, too, the only one in the Cotswolds, thought to be of Sir Giles de Berkeley, whose horse, Lombard, is also said to be buried in the churchyard.
Crickley Hill – Not only a good viewpoint but a centre in summer for an archaeological dig.

REFRESHMENTS:
Crickley Hill , during the summer only.
The Air Balloon (tel no: 0452 862541)

Walk 17   AROUND BOURTON-ON-THE-WATER   6½m (10km)
Maps: OS Sheets Landranger 163; Pathfinder SP 01/11.
A walk in the Windrush valley visiting a series of fine villages.
Start: At 178177, near New Bridge on a minor road towards
Clapton-on-the-Hill.

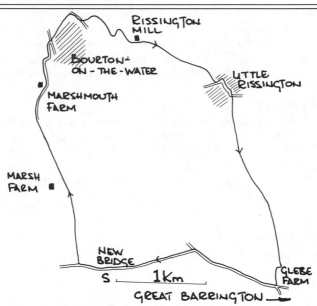

From the bridge over the Windrush walk up towards Clapton for about 300 yards and
then take the bridleway right. This is a well-used path and your general direction is
north towards **Bourton-on-the-Water**. Go across four fields towards a small farm,
passing a barn to go through a gate on to a road. Proceed on the road past two farms –
Marsh and Marshmouth – to Nethercote. At Marshmouth Farm there is a signpost
saying 'Little Rissington 2½ miles as the crow flies', with a crow on the top!

Continue on the road, passing Birdland, to reach a main road by a car park. If you
need refreshment, or want to visit, then go left into Bourton. Otherwise turn right. After
25 yards turn left by the signpost on to a footpath with tennis courts on the left. At the
end of the courts go over a stile on the right giving access to a path behind the changing
rooms. Continue ahead to a road: turn right. After about 200 yards you will come to two

gates, use the one on the right and, a few yards further on, take the footpath to the right between ponds. Follow the left pond right round to a stile in a hedge.

Go over this stile into a field and cross to another stile. Cross over this and head 45 degrees right across the field to a stream which you follow and cross by two bridges by Rissington Mill. Go out on to the road, turn right and on to where the road bends right. Cross the stile on the left and continue ahead on a well-walked path up the slope, crossing three fields to arrive at a wicket gate by **Little Rissington** Church. Go through and use the path through shrubbery round to the main church entrance. Go up to the main road, turn left and follow the road round right and up to a crossroads by Badgers Bank and Manor Farm.

Go straight ahead on to a bridleway and follow this for about 1 mile. At the bottom of a descent pass through a gate and follow the hedge, right, to another gate. Go through and continue following the hedge right. Go forward along the bottom of the field to the far corner and turn right through a wicket gate. Go down a few yards to a gate, turn left and go across the field to the farm buildings, keeping to the right to reach the main road in **Great Rissington**. Turn right. If you are thirsty the Lamb Inn is straight ahead, about 200 yards.

When refreshed, go down the road and after about $^1/_2$ mile turn left to New Bridge and the start of the walk.

POINTS OF INTEREST:

Bourton-on-the-Water – There is much to see in this famous village including Birdland and the model village.

Little and Great Rissington – Two typical Cotswold villages set on the hillside overlooking a Windrush valley. St Peter's Church, Little Rissington dates from the 12th century, although it was 'restored' in the 19th century. Men from RAF Little Rissington are buried on the eastern side of the graveyard. Both the altar cross and one of the windows are reminders of the village's long association with the RAF.

REFRESHMENTS:

Many places available in Bourton-on-the-Water.
The Lamb Inn, (tel no: 0451 20724)

Walk 18   DOWDESWELL RESERVOIR   6¹/₂m (10km)

Maps: OS Sheets Landranger Sheet 163; Pathfinder SO 81/91 and SO 82/92.

A walk in countryside on the fringe of Cheltenham.

Start: At 996196, in Little Herberts Road, Charlton Kings, near the old railway bridge.

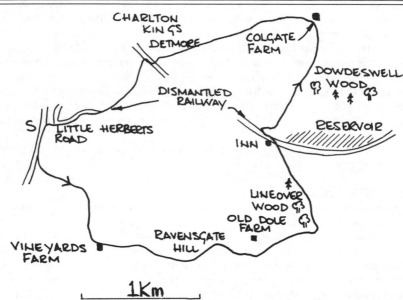

Walk uphill on the lane-cum-bridleway, signposted within about 100 yards to Wistley Hill. Fork right-handed through the wood, continue uphill on the well-defined track and, just before it enters Vineyards Farm, turn left through a gate in the fence. Immediately beyond, turn right on a footpath which becomes a track through a small wood and, just before reaching a large fuel storage tank, turn left across a field and through a gate. Here take the middle track of three, downhill with a hedge on your left and the grass escarpment on your right. As you pass through the next gate pick up the Cotswold Way waymarks (yellow arrow and white dot) which will assist you over the next two miles. Go straight ahead, keeping to the right of the farm buildings which you can see ahead, over a stile and take the right fork through the wood. On emerging, bear half-left across the corner of the field, go over the waymarked stile. Keep to the right, now, downhill past a fenced larch plantation, over a dismantled railway track to reach the A40 road. Immediately opposite is the pumphouse of **Dowdeswell Reservoir**, and if you wish to see the reservoir turn right around the bend.

Otherwise, turn left, past the Reservoir Inn (unless you wish to take refreshment, of course) and about 50 yards on turn very sharp right on a good track, to pass below the reservoir dam, passing the sluice and going up a track by the side of a forest plantation. Note the occasional information boards in the forest identifying various plantings. Also, keep a look out for jays and woodpeckers. Shortly after the track veers to the left away from the woodland you will meet a cross-track. Turn left, under power lines, to Colgate Farm. At this point you leave the Cotswold Way. Go through the farmyard into a field with scrub woodland on your right, and when that ends go straight ahead along the ridge, following a footpath through three fields – just skirting woodland on your left in the third field – descending all the way to a stile on the left side of farm buildings at Detmore. Follow the direction indicated by the footpath finger post across the field, making for a large tree. Behind this cross the footbridge. Go right along the bank of the brook into a lane, and turn left to reach the A40 again. Turn right, and immediately after Balcarras Lawn Hotel turn left up the track, over stiles through two fields to join a lane. Here, turn left through the gate and immediately right alongside the hedge, over a stile and into The Beeches housing estate. Follow the road, turning left into Ravensgate Road and along an alley by the side of Number 29 into Little Herberts Road again. Turn left to your car or right to the bus stop.

POINTS OF INTEREST:
Dowdeswell Reservoir – Provides water for Cheltenham. You may not enter the grounds, but in the spring rhododendrons on the far shore beneath the trees make a beautiful picture.

REFRESHMENTS:
The Reservoir Inn, Dowdeswell (tel no: 0242 529671).

Maps: OS Sheets Landranger 150; Pathfinder SP 03/13.

A lovely scarp edge walk with extensive panoramic views.

Start: Buckland village, off the Cheltenham road south of Broadway.

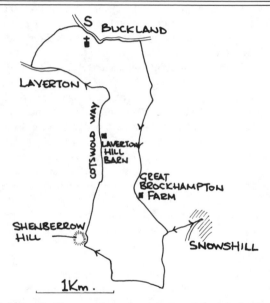

Proceed up the **Buckland** village road past the church and up to the holiday flats. Keep to the road and climb up the side of the valley past a trout farm and up to level. Continue on road to some farm buildings. Proceed ahead passing through a gate and make for another gate up to your left between woods. This gives access to a well-defined track.

This track goes right round the hill past Brockhampton Farm for about 1 mile towards **Snowshill.** On reaching the road, turn left down to the village if you are in need of refreshment. Leave Snowshill by the same road and retrace your steps. Go up the slope out of the village and go right on the minor road to where you came from Buckland. Now go straight on and then take the bridleway left after 200 yards towards some barns. Follow arrows around the buildings and go through a gate into a field. Walk along the track, following a fence and broken wall on the right, and proceed to the road.

Pass through the gate at the roadside, turn immediately right and in 10 yards turn right into a copse. Continue ahead and go up to a field, keeping to the track on the right. Climb to the top and at the cross-tracks turn right through a gate. Cross two fields and turn left on to a definite track across to Shenberrow Hill (see Walk 15). Follow the track round farm buildings to the right, through a gate and on to a good single road.

This is the Cotswold Way: turn right and follow the yellow arrows with a white dot. After about $^1/_2$ mile cross a cattle grid and follow the Cotswold Way round left. (Do not follow the first track left to Stanton.) Follow the track past Laverton Hill Barn and continue forward until you start to descend. At this point there are some beech trees where you turn left down another track – not the Cotswold Way – to Laverton. Proceed downhill to the village. Pass through a gate at the bottom and on to the road. Where the main road comes in from the left, turn right on to a footpath opposite. This is a good hard path back to Buckland.

POINTS OF INTEREST:
Buckland – Famous for its Rectory.
Snowshill – A beautiful hill-set village. The Manor, owned by the National Trust, is well worth a visit.

REFRESHMENTS:
The Snowshill Arms (tel no: 0386 852653).

Walk 20   COBERLEY AND ELKSTONE   7m (11km)

Maps: OS Sheets Landranger 163; Pathfinder SO 81/91.

A walk on the hillsides of the Churn valley .

Start: At 968143, the Green Dragon pub, Cockleford.

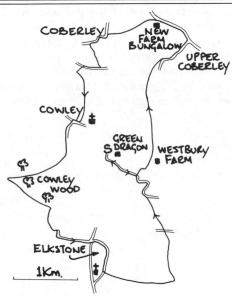

Turn left uphill and after 100 yards turn left (signposted 'Cockleford – No Through
Road'). After 500 yards go left down beside 'The Cottage, Cockleford' to the River
Churn. Cross the bridge and pass in front of a house and up its driveway to the A435.
Cross over to the lane marked for 'Westbury Farm'. This is a good track going uphill
and bending left to arrive, after just over 1 mile, at a road in Upper Coberley. At this
road, turn right and go through the hamlet to the top of the hill. At the T-junction turn
left for New Farm Bungalow about 500 yards along on the left-hand side. You will see
a footpath sign here: go between the buildings and, with a hedge on the left, go down
two fields, through a wicket gate (bottom left) and down a steep bank to the road, the
A435. Cross to the road, to Coberley (see Walk 16) and go ahead to the church.

   Coberley Church is worth a visit, but the walk turns left into a field just before the
buildings. Pass behind the church, crossing the field to a gate into a wood. A short track

between gates takes you into a field which you cross to the taller trees opposite. Pass through a gate on to a track and turn right down to a cottage. Go up to the building and then, by keeping left and passing some delightful water gardens, go around to the rear and on to a green track. At this point go left over a stile into a field and ahead to the trees. Cross the footbridge over the stream, go up the bank, turn right and, at a facing hedge, turn left with the hedge on your right for 150 yards. Cut through the hedge and go across the field, veering slightly right to a stile in the facing fence. Cross over this and another field to a stile and a well-groomed grass path which takes you to **Cowley**.

Continue ahead past the Manor and follow the road right. Fork left by Scraggs Farm and left again by the memorial. After $^2/_3$ mile, having gone up the valley and through trees, look for a road sharp left near the top of the rise. This goes to farm buildings. At the wall in front of a wood, turn right. Go ahead with the wall and wood on the left. Cross two fields and, just past a gate into the wood, turn right in front of the wall. Go to an old gateway at the end of the wall, cut through, follow a hedge and then a wall on the right to the road. Go left to a junction. Turn right into a minor road and follow this to a crossroads. Cross over to **Elkstone** and follow the road round, through the village, passing the school on the left.

Continue to the Mill House, on the left, and just around the corner a path right, by a wall, leads to the church, which is worth a visit. The walk, however, continues on a track going to the left by Mill House. Go past a pond, left, and up a bank to a beech copse. Fork right and cross the field to a gate. Go through, turn right and go ahead to a wood. Turn left down the valley forking left at the end of the wood. Go down to the bottom right corner, turn left and go up the valley through a gate to reach a road at the top, following the hedge on the right. Cross the road and go through a gate into a field. Make for the trees ahead. Keep left and go down to the hedge and through the gate in the corner. Veer left in the next field and shortly you will see a gate by fence posts. Go through and down the track to a gate and the road. Turn left and return to the start.

POINTS OF INTEREST:

Cowley – Cowley Manor was built by Sir John Horlick and is now owned by Gloucestershire CC. The gardens with some lovely lakes are open to the public. The 12th-century church, St Mary's, stands in the Manor grounds, by the river.

Elkstone – The Norman church has a dovecote above the chancel reached by a newel stairway near the pulpit.

REFRESHMENTS:

The Green Dragon, Cockleford (tel no: 024287 271).

Maps: OS Sheets Landranger 163; Pathfinder SP 02/12.
A pleasant walk on the hills above Naunton.
Start: The Black Horse pub in Naunton.

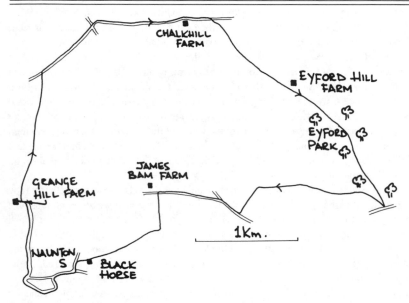

Walk west on the road through Naunton (see Walk 13) to the village hall, turn left down the road opposite the hall and descend to the River Windrush. Cross over the river, go through a gate and turn right. Note the 17th-century dovecote on your right.

Proceed along the field following the track to a gate. Pass through on to the road and walk along to the main road. Turn right. Re-cross the river and take the left fork. Climb for $^1/_2$ mile to reach Grange Hill Farm and at the crossroads go straight across on to a track. Continue ahead and in $^3/_4$ mile you will reach another road: turn right and go ahead for $^1/_2$ mile to a crossroads. Cross over to the Lower Swell road and proceed for nearly 1 mile. When in a wooded area look for the 'Private Road' to Eyford Park on the right. This is a public bridleway.

Turn right on to this road. Your way now lies through Eyford Park. The road becomes a track and then a road again, but keep straight ahead for about $1^3/_4$ miles.

When you come to the main Swell road, turn right and almost immediately right again before a row of houses to enter fields. Pass through the gate and follow the track left up the slope to a gate at the top. Go forward across two fields towards barns. Go through the gates and turn left, following the hedge, to the road. Cross over, go through a gate and turn sharp right to follow the wall round. Continue ahead now for about $^1/_2$ mile with the wall and road on your right to James Barn Farm. Opposite the farm turn left down the field to the bottom left corner and follow the path, now going right between bushes, up a bank and across the field. Cross two more fields and enter a coppice. Go straight on down to Naunton and the start of the walk.

REFRESHMENTS:
The Black Horse, Naunton (tel no: 04515 378)

Walk 22 HARFORD BRIDGE AND THE SLAUGHTERS 7m (11km)

Maps: OS Sheets Landranger 163; Pathfinder SP 02/12.

A walk down the Windrush Valley with the return through the famous Slaughter villages.

Start: At 128228, Harford Bridge on the B4068.

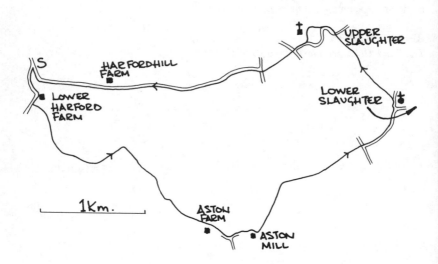

Take the road from the crossroads near the bridge marked 'Lower Harford Farm only' and go down $\frac{1}{4}$ mile to the river. Cross at the ford and go ahead on the road 100 yards and then over a stile on the left into a field. Cross this to another gate, pass through and walk beside the river across two fields before coming to a field with steep slopes covered with gorse and hawthorn. Following the blue arrows, climb the bank to a facing fence, turn right and follow the edge of the wood. Enter the wood by a gate in the corner and keeping the same direction for $\frac{1}{2}$ mile, passing a railway bridge in a dip, you will come to a field planted with sage bushes at the time of writing. Cross the field to farm buildings (Aston Farm), and follow arrows down to the road. Turn left to Aston Mill House with its attractive gardens and collection of birds. Pass in front of the house up to a gate. Go through and turn left on to a track signposted 'The Slaughters'. Go up through this wooded area to a gate and enter a field. Once again, cross to another gate and in 75 yards leave this track to go right through a gate and across to the road. Cross over on to another track for $^1/_4$ mile and at the next road cross over on to the road down into **Lower Slaughter**.

When you reach the river running through this picturesque village, cross over the road and use the bridge on the left to go towards a water-wheel. Pass round in front of the Post Office and look for a path between buildings past Colletts, the bakery. Keep straight ahead through two kissing gates and on to a path beside the river. Look out for mallard ducks and herons here. Go through a gate and cross four fields to the road down towards Upper Slaughter. The river and gardens (including a small water-wheel) at the Lords of the Manor Hotel are worth viewing.

Reaching the road, turn left into **Upper Slaughter** and, on arriving at the river's edge, look for a seat. There is a path beside the river for 150 yards upstream to a ford. At this point, turn left up to a telephone kiosk and go past the church on the right and on to the main road beside a traffic island with three trees on it. Turn right uphill to a T-junction and opposite is a field gate giving access to a track up a slope. Proceed on this, with a wall on your right, up to the top. Pass through two gates and on to a road beside cottages. Cross over to the road signposted 'Lower Harford' and continue down the road past Hill Farm. After 1 mile you will come back to the start of the walk.

POINTS OF INTEREST:

The Slaughters – The name probably means 'The place of the Sloes'. These picturesque villages attract, quite rightly, thousands of visitors in the summer. Find some time to wander around beside the River Eye.

REFRESHMENTS:
Numerous in both villages.

Walk 23   AROUND WITHINGTON   7¹/₂m (12km)

Maps: OS Sheets Landranger 163; Pathfinder SP 01/11.

With good observation this ramble can be very rewarding.

Start: At 038133, near Chedworth Airfield.

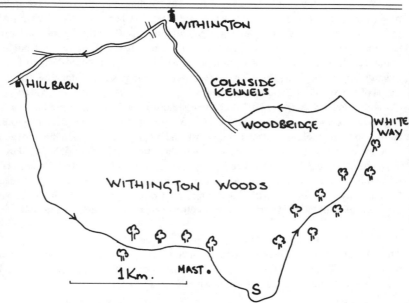

Park at the old aerodrome and take the road through Withington Wood towards Cassey Compton. After 1 mile you will pass over the old Chedworth railway – the bridge is quite obvious on a flatter part of the descent. As the road goes on down, look for a footpath sign on the left bank. Go over the stile into a steep field. Follow the track down the field to the right and, when convenient, walk to the left far corner of the field and a gate. Pass through, cross over the stream and go over the stile on the right. Ascend towards the road to a gate, pass through and turn left. With a hedge on the left proceed to the next stile. Now follow the contour of the bank and the pylons for about ¹/₂ mile over more stiles – there are waymarks. When you come to some buildings on the left start moving slightly right towards a gate in front of the old railway. Pass through the gate, under the railway and on to the road. Turn right towards Withington. Pass Colnside Kennels and then, where the road runs under a bridge, look for a footpath sign by a renovated cottage on the left. Follow this path, beside a stream, to **Withington** where you emerge between buildings opposite the Mill Inn – time for refreshment. As an alternative the King's Head is up the road to the right.

When ready, continue to the left, up the slope. Take the Colesbourne road opposite the church and climb the hill using the narrow road, keeping left where the road forks to Hilcot. As the road levels out look for Hill Barn on your left. In front of this is a very clear bridleway going south-west. Using this you now walk nearly 2 miles across the top of the hill with Withington Wood to the left. At first there is a slight descent and then a rise to a short stretch of woodland from which you emerge into a field where pheasants are bred. Continue and re-enter woodland, at first scrub, and you will pass a cottage on your right before coming to a TV relay station by a road. Cross the road to a field gate, slightly right, and enter the field with a wall to the left. After 150 yards enter the wood by a gate and follow the path to the right. Where the path turns left, pass over a stile and into a field, between fences, and back to the start.

POINTS OF INTEREST:
Withington – A fine village with a good church. The River Coln flows through the village.
Deer can be seen anywhere on this walk, if you are lucky.

REFRESHMENTS:
The Mill Inn, Withington (tel no: 024289 204)
The Kings Head, Withington (tel no: 024289 216)

Walk 24 ALSTONE, OXENTON AND WOOLSTONE 7¹/₂m (12km)

Maps: OS Sheets Landranger 150, Pathfinder SO 83/93.

A moderately demanding walk through pleasant countryside.

Start: At 990332, the A438 lay-by a short distance west of the Hobnails Inn.

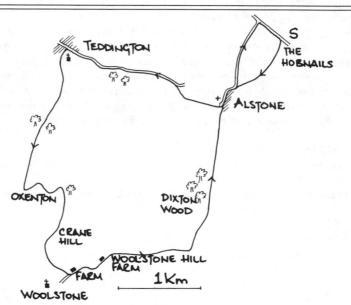

Cross over the stile almost opposite the Hobnails Inn and walk with the hedge on your right. Go over two stiles through a small plantation, keep to the right in the next field, over another stile and through a gap in the hedge on your right where there is a waymark sign. Continue with the hedge on your left to reach a road and turn left into **Alstone**. Take the second left and, after passing the church, turn right by the telephone kiosk into fields, keeping the fence on your right. After the next stile, walk with the hedge on your left, cross two stiles through a wide hedge and turn right to a gate into a lane. Turn left and enter Teddington. Take the second left (a cul de sac), and at the end cross a stile. Follow the left-hand boundary of the field uphill, go over another stile and immediately through a gate on the right. Turn left, keeping the hedge on your left for 50 yards, then bear diagonally right-handed across the field to a large tree in the top corner. Cross the stile into a wood, and follow a muddy track up a bank through scrub into open ground. Keep the wood on your left until you come to the corner of a field on your right.

Cross the stile and go diagonally left across the corner of the field to reach a stile in the hedge ahead. Cross and go half-right downhill to the church and to the road. **Oxenton** is to the right; however, turn left and go through a farm gate up a wide track with a fence on the right. Go through another farm gate and follow the wide track to the right and up the bank to another gate giving access to a wood. Go through the wood into a field, then straight ahead over a stile into the next field. Here, at first, keep the fence on your right but where it turns sharply away to the right continue straight across the field to a stile by a gate in the far fence. Cross the stile, go straight ahead for about ten yards, then follow a path bearing away to the right around Crane Hill, converging gradually on the fence on your right, after which descend to cross a stile in the bottom corner of the field. Go through the farmyard, turn left on to the lane, and straight ahead to Woolstone Hill Farm. Do not enter the farm but turn right alongside farm buildings to pass through a gate into fields.

Turn left and then right to follow the overhead power cables through three fields, at which point leave the cables to bear slightly left across the next two fields via waymarked stiles (the second of these is located between two old willows). Bear half-left and uphill to a metal farm gate in the far hedge near a small hawthorn plantation. Skirt Dixton Wood on your left but where it sweeps away uphill continue straight on gradually downhill along a line of single trees (once part of a hedge). Go over the stile ahead and cross the ditch by a wooden bridge, along the side of a barn. Go over two stiles close together, making first for a single tree protected by a paling fence to a final stile in the far hedge. Cross over, keep to the right, and re-enter Alstone at the telephone kiosk you passed earlier in the walk. Turn left and then right on public roads to join the A438 and collect your car.

POINTS OF INTEREST:
Oxenton Church – St John Baptist, 13/14/15th-century, tower uncommonly enclosed within nave. Elizabethan carved oak communion table and some murals.
Woolstone Church – St Martin, 14/15th century. Unusual 14th-century font.
Alstone Church – St Margaret, Norman origin, wooden bell turret.

REFRESHMENTS:
The Hobnails Inn, Alderton (tel no: 024262 458).

Walk 25   DUMBLETON TO ALDERTON   8m (13km)

Maps: OS Sheets Landranger 150; Pathfinder SP 03/13.

A walk over hills which give glorious views.

Start: At 018358, in front of the Edward Holland monument in Dumbleton.

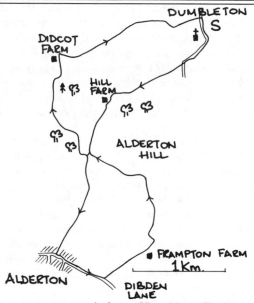

Leave the monument to pass in front of Dumbleton Church and go round to the right across the driveway of Dumbleton Hall and on to the 'No Through Road'. Follow this for 250 yards and then take the bridleway right marked 'Alderton'. Follow this all the way up to Hill Farm – seen at the head of the valley – passing Dumbleton Hall to the right with its lovely gardens containing many flowering shrubs. Having reached the top, pass to the left of Hill Farm and cross the field to a wood. Pass through a gateway and in 50 yards follow the Alderton sign right and in a further 25 yards descend down a gully. Where the track turns left, go through a gate right and into a field. Following the hedge left, descend through fields towards Alderton, seen in front – about $^1/_2$ mile away.

Nearing the first house, cross a stile and follow the fence left across a paddock to another stile. Cross this and go down the path to the main road – the Gardener's Arms is about 300 yards to the right. Return to the point where you reached the road and go left along Beckford Road and, keeping left, go into Dibden Lane. Proceed ahead and leave Alderton. About 400 yards beyond the last house, at the dip in the road, look for a stile on the left. Cross this and go diagonally right across a field towards Frampton Farm. The next stile to look for is on the left of the farm buildings roughly in line with overhead wires crossing the fields. The stile is waymarked, with a yellow arrow and black dot. Continue slightly left to a track on the far side of the next field. At the footpath sign turn left along a green track which then turns right after approximately 100 yards. Follow the track up the field to arrive at a gate by a wood.

Go through the gate and with the wood on your right proceed ahead up the field. Nearing the top of this field, turn left on to a track. Follow this to an iron gate. You are now on the Wychavon Way. Pass through a gate into a wood and at a junction of tracks follow the main track round to the right. In a few more yards you will arrive at a gateway to a field. Turn left here on to path marked with 'W' sign, still inside the wood. Follow this round to a track, and turn right, still following the edge of the wood.

At the point where there is a gate on the right for entry into a field, turn left and go straight down the bank following the 'W' signs through the wood. You will emerge at a gate at the top of a field with Didcot Farm at the bottom. Follow the boundary left and descend towards the farm, looking for a stile in the fence left near buildings. Do not go over the stile, but leave the Wychavon Way here to turn right. With the farm now left, follow the yellow arrows with black dots. Cross the stile by the gate and go over to the facing hedge. Cross over the footbridge and go up the bank to re-enter the wood by a gate on the right. Once in the wood, turn left, and follow a path round to a facing gate. Pass through into a field. Still with the wood to your right, proceed ahead to the right corner of the field. Pass over a double stile to re-enter the wood and in a short distance cross another stile into a field. Your path lies 45 degrees right, but a fence faces you down to a gate at the bottom of the field. Turn right and find the stile you should have crossed! Turn left across the field and aim for the cricket field to go over a stile in the fence. Turn left and go down Dairy Lane to the road, and then turn right back to the starting point.

REFRESHMENTS:

The Gardener's Arms, Alderton (tel no: 024262 257).

Walk 26   KILKENNY TO DOWDESWELL   8m (13km)

Maps: OS Sheets Landranger 163; Pathfinder SP 01/11.

A fine walk with excellent views.

Start: At 004185, the car park at the Kilkenny picnic area.

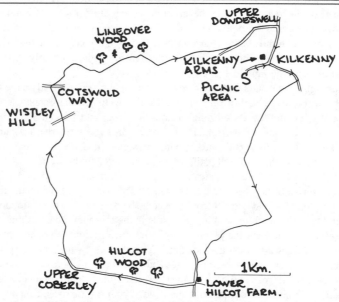

Leave the car park and walk down to the A436. Turn right and walk down to the Kilkenny Arms pub and then take the Foxcote road to the right. After 400 yards take the bridleway right, which climbs gradually out of the valley past Cabin Farm for about 1 mile. Follow this path to the top with fine views back down to Foxcote and across the valley to the Shiptons. Reaching the facing wall at the top, turn left and follow the wall across two fields. When you reach the field gate under three electric wires and by a fir copse, go through the gate and turn immediately right through a second gate. Follow the track to the left. Continue ahead down the field, through a gate and on to a stile in the left corner of the next field. Go over this and in 150 yards cross a stile in a fence and go down a steep bank to arrive at a black and white house on the roadside.

    Turn left on the road and continue forward to the crossroads where you turn right to Upper Coberley. Do not go into the hamlet but keep right and in 150 yards take the

Wistley Hill track to the right. Go to the top of the field, keep right in the next field and make for a wooded headland. At this point look for the black and white markers and go across the field to the left. If you miss the markers go round the field anti-clockwise to arrive at a wicket gate in the far corner by a power cable tower. Pass through the gate and follow the path with a hedge on the right up to Chatcombe Wood. In $^3/_4$ mile you will reach the A436. Cross over. You are now on the Cotswold Way, so follow the yellow arrows with the white dot. Cross the field, go through a plantation into a field at the top of a steep bank. There are wonderful views from here.

Following the arrows, go down the steep bank and across, eastwards to Lineover Wood. In approximately $^1/_2$ mile you emerge from the wood into a field where you leave the Cotswold Way. Go up the field to the right to arrive at some gates. Do not go through but follow the track down left to a barn. Passing it on the right, go along the track to Dowdeswell. Pass the manor house, an old fountain and a telephone box and come to a road. Turn right up to the Kilkenny Arms and from here turn right back up to the start of the walk.

REFRESHMENTS:
The Kilkenny Arms (tel no: 0242 820341).

Walks 27 and 28   **BLOCKLEY AND BATSFORD**   8m (13km)

Maps: OS Sheets Landranger 151; Pathfinder SP 03/13.

A walk through undulating countryside, which may be shortened to 5 miles if you wish.

Start: At 164356, the car park at the sports field in Blockley.

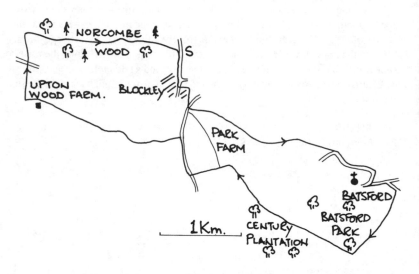

From the car park turn right, passing a long terrace of Cotswold stone cottages on the left, to the British Legion Hall. Go through the churchyard, turn right on to the B4479 and, just past Brook House Hotel, go left into a lane, over a cattle grid, and up a gentle slope. When the track sweeps away to the left go on up the right side of the field passing between a barn and a hedge. Go through a gate and up towards the crest, bearing slightly left to keep a hedge, and then a wood, on the right. Where the wood ends, go through a gate, walk with the wall/hedge on your left and in the second field bear half-right on a track across the field to join a road at the end of the hedge on the far side. Walk down to a crossroads. Turn right through **Batsford** to a T-junction. Turn left down a tree-lined avenue and, in about 100 yards, go right on to a bridleway between fences, at the end of which cross a stile on the right. Follow a path, with a field boundary first on your left and then on your right, across six fields. Along this section you will get a fine view on your right of Batsford village and the big house at Batsford Park. Soon the boundary on your right will be marked by a wall. Where it ends, go through a gate, then turn right across a field to pass to the left of a Cotswold stone lodge. Go over a stile, cross a private road, go through the gate opposite, and cross a field to a gate into the wood ahead. Turn right and then left on to an unmetalled drive, ascending gently for 300 yards until the drive swings to the left, at which point turn right on to a waymarked path to the park wall a few yards away. Go up the path with the wall on your right and Century Plantation on your left, until the park wall ends. Cross a road and continue over two fields, keeping the hedge left, before turning left on a cross-track through scrub.

To shorten the walk look out for a stile on your right and a waymarked path which goes back to Blockley (see Walk 14), clearly visible below. Otherwise, go straight on and, at a road, go right for 300 yards, then left into a lane opposite a sign offering bed and breakfast accommodation at Park Farm. When the lane steepens, go left on a narrow, metalled path to join a road. Turn left and, very shortly, right on a track beside a letter box. When the track forks, take the right-hand option, passing a large house on the right, through a gate into woodland. Ascend gradually through woods, ignoring alternative routes, until your track converges on a field to the left. Go through the gate here and cross the field with the woods on your right for a short distance, continuing over another field to pass right of **Upton Wold Farm,** and along the farm drive. At the first field wall turn right on to a crossing path keeping the wall/hedge on your right. Cross a road, go straight ahead to enter Norcombe Wood, and at the valley bottom turn right into the woodland ride. When the track divides into three, follow the left-hand one, ignoring side tracks, until it leaves the wood. The path becomes a little indistinct here, so steer a course half-right up the steeply banked field to the far end of a line of trees on the crest. The sports field will be ahead, and your car will be reached by following the boundary fence to the left.

POINTS OF INTEREST:

Batsford – Batsford Park was originally the seat of Baron Redesdale, whose famous daughters, the Mitford girls, intrigued the world with their exploits. Now a famous Arboretum and garden centre, both worth a visit. Also worthwhile is St Mary's Church.
Upton Wold Farm – Superb 17th-century Manor House.

REFRESHMENTS:
The Crown Inn, Blockley (tel no: 0386 700245).
The Great Western Arms, Blockley (tel no: 0386 700362).

Walk 29 COLESBOURNE TO SEVEN SPRINGS 8m (13km)

Maps: OS Sheets Landranger 163; Pathfinder SO 81/91.

A lovely walk in the Churn Valley.

Start: At 985141, on the minor road from Colesbourne to Hilcot, just by a wood with a track below it.

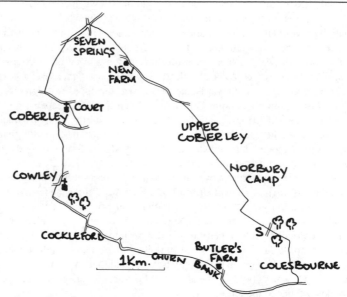

Take the track north-west past a white barn. At the end of the wood, right, turn right along a less well-defined track, but still with the wood on your right. At the top of the incline turn left, following the right boundary. Still climbing you will reach some beech trees, the site of Norbury Camp. Although it is 2,500 years old, the camp's ditches and banks can still be seen. Continue ahead between trees towards another wood. Drop down to a gateway and a cottage on your left and, still proceeding north-west, leave the wood and cross a field to the Coberley-Hilcot road. Turn left and, at the next fork, turn right. As the road starts to descend by New Farm, take the bridleway right towards a small wood. Continue down to **Seven Springs** crossroads and cross over the A435 to the A436 towards Gloucester. The Seven Springs Inn is on your left and the actual springs to your right where the old road bends round the back. Go past the springs to a stile, left. Cross a field to a stile in the facing hedge. Turn left and follow the path and track to Coberley village (see Walk 16). Keeping left of the school and the obelisk, go down to the main road and bear left for 400 yards to the church. The church is behind the buildings on the roadside and access is through a small door in the wall, as directed. At the end of the buildings, take the marked footpath right, go behind the church across a field to a gate and pass through to a facing wood. A short track between gates now takes you into a field which you cross to the taller trees opposite. Pass through a gate on to a track and turn right down to a cottage. Your path leads up to the building and then, by keeping left, past some delightful water gardens and round to the start of a green track. At this point look for a stile left to go over into the next field, and cross this by following the fence to a small footbridge over a stream.

Go up the bank, turn right to the corner of the field, then left with the hedge on your right. After 150 yards, pass through a gap in the hedge and go diagonally across the field, making for a stile in the fence. Go over, cross another field and stile to a well-groomed grass path, with a house on the left, leading to a road. Continue ahead past Cowley Manor (see Walk 20) and, after a bend in the road by a telephone box, look for the road to the Green Dragon Inn, Cockleford, on the left. Turn right at the inn and after 100 yards take the road left marked 'Cockleford – No Through Road'. At Churn Bank you will pass through a gate into a field. Keeping to this direction, pass through another gate into a field where the path crosses to the other side of the hedge you have been following. Keep going ahead to Butler's Farm where, at the road, you turn right. At the crossroads by Penhill Farm keep ahead and follow the road to Colesbourne.

At the A435 continue ahead to the Colesbourne Inn and, at the end of the inn's car park, look for a track to the left. Go down this, over the River Churn, and straight up the slope to a field ahead, passing cottages on the left. Enter the field but turn right through a gateway. Turning left immediately, climb the bank with a hedge on your left, ignoring the kissing gate half-way up, and on the level you will find a metal gate leading into a wood. Pass through on to a green track between trees and after 350 yards you will pass between two stone pillars on to the road at the start of the walk.

POINTS OF INTEREST:
Seven Springs – The source of the River Churn, a tributary of the River Thames.

REFRESHMENTS:
Seven Springs Inn (tel no: 024287 385).
The Green Dragon, Cockleford (tel no: 024287 271).
Colesbourne Inn (tel no: 024287 376).

Walk 30   **AROUND MICKLETON**   8$\frac{1}{2}$m (13.5km)

Maps: OS Sheets Landranger 151; Pathfinder SP 04/14.

A walk in the north Cotswolds, passing two houses open to the public in the summer.

Start: At 162435, in the lane near the church in Mickleton.

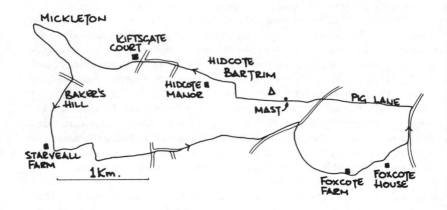

Pass **Mickleton** Church by and go right, up a bank to a kissing gate and into a field. Cross this at about 45 degrees right to a gate at the edge of a thicket. Pass through, go over the stream and through shrubbery to another gate giving access to a field. Keeping the hedge on the left, go straight up the slope to another gate. Pass through and go right, climbing up to a road. Cross over on to a bridleway up a bank and then turn right 200 yards round the edge of the field to enter the wood. This is Baker's Hill. Follow the path through the trees at the top of a bank and maintain the direction to reach Starveall Farm. Turn left and cross the road to the hedge opposite. With the hedge on your right descend the field to a footbridge at the bottom. Follow the waymark arrows to the left, around the field to a point opposite where you entered the field, by a pylon. A few yards further on turn left through a gate to walk another 250 yards to the road.

This is Hidcote Boyce. Go straight over and through the hamlet to where the road turns right by a farm. Keep ahead on a track, cross the field and then go up a slope where the track starts to bend right towards an old quarry and barns in a hollow. Go through a gate set in a stone wall, seen above the barns. Proceed to another road, cross straight over and after approximately 500 yards, where the road bends left, take the bridleway right. (There is a notice asking for dogs to be kept on leads here.) Follow the track, with trees left and a view across the valley. As pheasants are bred here you could see a lot of them about. Continue ahead and after crossing a stile you will see Foxcote Farm down the hill. The next gate you want is by the farm, so go straight down to it.

Pass through this gate on to a road, turn left and proceed to Foxcote Manor. At the far entrance to the house take the road slightly left and continue to the main road. Turn left and after 400 yards you will find a track to the left which is known as Pig Lane. Take this. (At the top of the slope a track leads down to the Dunstall Building – a rather elegant barn. This is not on our walk but is worth a visit.)

The walk continues along Pig Lane passing the radar masts to a road. Turn left and after a few yards turn right through a gateway into a field. Turn right following the boundary to the booster station. Pass this by to the left and follow the track for about $^{1}/_{2}$ mile to **Hidcote Bartrim**.

Pass through the car park and on to the road. Go straight down to the main road and cross over to take the path through a field down the slope beside the **Kiftsgate Court** entrance. This is a well-used path. Go down to the bottom and through a gate between trees. Then, keeping left, cross to another gate and follow the edge of the field to yet another gate. As the field opens up set a course for Mickleton church, a couple of fields away. At the right-hand edge of the church is a small gate, pass through and return to the start of the walk.

POINTS OF INTEREST:

Mickleton – Well worth a walk round.

Hidcote Bartrim – The Manor, now owned by the National Trust, is open during the summer.

Kiftsgate Court – Also open to the public on certain days during the summer.

Walk 31 YANWORTH TO CHEDWORTH ROMAN VILLA 9m (14km)

Maps: OS Sheets Landranger 163; Pathfinder SP 01/11.

A super ramble. Thoroughly recommended.

Start: At 072130, near the River Coln.

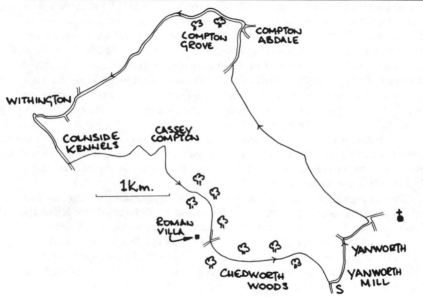

Climb up the hill to **Yanworth** and at the top turn right into the village. Go past the village hall to where the road turns right. At this point go left where a rough track marked 'Private Road' begins. If you wish to visit the church it is among the farm buildings down on your right. Otherwise, go up the track for nearly 1 mile and look for another track, left, with a wall on the left which heads north-west towards a copse. Continue to the road, then turn right and go down to **Compton Abdale.** At the crossroads look for the crocodile's head spewing water into a stream at the side of the road. Follow this road for two miles to Withington (see Walk 23). As you go down into the village, the King's Head public house is on your left and you could stop here or at the Mill Inn farther down on the right for refreshment.

Going on, there is a footpath sign opposite the Mill Inn which shows the Right of Way up some steps and between buildings to a path by the stream. Follow this and proceed through to a road. Turn right by a railway bridge and carry on past Colnside Kennels to the next bridge. There is a footpath sign and a stone carved 'Woodside'. Pass under the bridge to a gate. Go through the gate and forward a few yards and then turn 45 degrees right across the field. This is now the general direction as you proceed along the valley with a bank on your left. The path is well used and easy to follow over several stiles. After about $^1/_2$ mile it climbs to a stile in a stone wall. Go over and across the field with a hedge on the right to a gate at the far corner. Go through and descend to a stile and a footbridge over the stream at the bottom. Turn left through a field gate and follow the stream to the road. This is Cassey Compton. There is an interesting barn over on the left with other farm buildings.

Go to the nearby crossroads and go straight over to follow the River Coln. This is a delightful part of the walk where much wildlife can be seen, including pheasants and mallards. **Chedworth Woods** are on your right and after about 1 mile the road turns left over the Coln. On your right you can turn to walk about $^1/_4$ mile to **Chedworth Roman Villa**. Our walk continues straight ahead on to the 'Private Road' where there is a Right of Way for ramblers. After about 1 mile you will return to the starting point.

POINTS OF INTEREST:
Yanworth – A small village with its parish church set in a farmyard and surrounded with barns.
Compton Abdale – The church on the hill and the crocodile's head are interesting.
Chedworth Woods – There are wild deer in the woods.
Chedworth Roman Villa – Built in the early part of the second century AD and open to the public.

REFRESHMENTS:
The Mill Inn, Withington (tel no: 024289 204)
King's Head, Withington (tel no: 024289 216)
Chedworth Roman Villa (tel no: 024289 256)

Walk 32 SEVEN SPRINGS AND LECKHAMPTON HILL 9m (14km)
Maps: OS Sheets Landranger 163; Pathfinder SO 81/91.

An interesting walk with some excellent views.

Start: At 968171, Seven Springs at the crossroads of the A435 and A436.

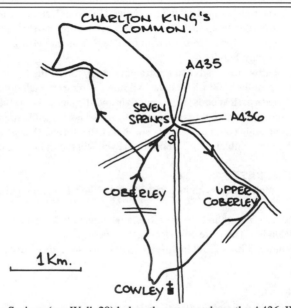

Start by the Springs (see Walk 29) below the crossroads on the A436. Walk up to the crossroads and immediately opposite is a bridleway. Take this to climb the hill and, where it levels off, join a road. Turn left and, at the next junction, turn right into Upper Coberley. Go down the hill through the hamlet between the converted farm buildings for $^2/_3$ mile to the main road (A435). Cross over to Cowley (see Walk 20). At the bottom of the slope go over the River Churn and now, on your left, you will see the start of Cowley Manor Gardens. Walking on up the slope, look for the pathway to Coberley on the right along a neatly-cut grass path. Arrows on the stiles point across the fields to Coberley. Cross two fields, then cut through a gap in the facing hedge. Turn left to the end of the field and then right, and after 100 yards, cross over the footbridge. Walk up the bank and into a field. Cross this to a green track and then cross, using two stiles into another field. Make a line across the field to Coberley (see Walk 16) which can be seen half-left. Go over a stile and up a bank to the road. Turn right and then immediately left, passing an obelisk on your left. Pass a school and then ahead you will see a sign and a track to Seven Springs and Leckhampton Hill. Follow this track, between hedges, up to a field. If you wish to return to Seven Springs at this point follow the path ahead until you reach a stile on the right. Cross this and walk between fences back to the starting point.

To continue the walk, on entering the field on the track from Coberley turn left with a hedge on your left. Where the hedge turns downhill, continue ahead to a facing hedge and then turn right up to the road (A436). Go straight over the road with the golf course on the left and continue ahead on a bridleway. It dips down, then climbs to a wood on the right before descending to a gateway. Go through, turn left to the top of the field and then turn right under power lines to the end of the field. Turn left through a gap in the hedge and follow the track with a wall on the right to the minor road at the top. You are now on the Cotswold Way. Follow the direction of a white arrow on the ash tree down the road for 250 yards to a quarry. Turn right on the top side and follow the markers (yellow arrows with white dot). Look out for the Devil's Chimney (see Walk 5) on your left at the top of the slope. From here, and for quite a distance, there are sensational views across Cheltenham towards the Welsh hills and the Malverns. This is common land controlled by Cheltenham Corporation and leads to Charlton Kings Common. There are numerous paths criss-crossing the land but if you follow the edge of the escarpment you cannot go wrong (about 2 miles). The whole area is covered by gorse bushes – quite a sight when they are in flower.

Still following the Cotswold Way, go down off the escarpment and cross a field to reach a minor road. Continue ahead to the Seven Springs crossroads and the starting point of the walk.

REFRESHMENTS:

Seven Springs Inn (tel no: 024287 385).

Walk 33   **WILLERSEY TO BROADWAY**   9m (14.5km)

Maps: OS Sheets Landranger 150; Pathfinder SP 03/13.

Two hills and three fine villages make this a perfect walk.

Start: At Willersey church.

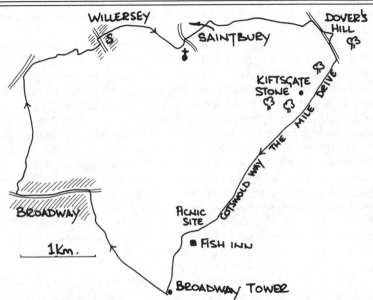

Facing St Peter's Church, **Willersey**, go through the gate beside the memorial and veer left through a wicket gate into a field. Keep right to the bottom of the field and go over a stile and stone footbridge into the next field. In 25 yards, go left over a double stile and bridge and cross to a wicket gate and on to a track. After another 25 yards go right over a stile into a field. Veer left to a gate to another field. With the hedge and fence on your left, go up towards Saintbury church. At the top, turn left, and pass over a stile by a cottage and below the church. Go on to a tarmac path and turn left down to the road. Turn right uphill and in 25 yards take the path left past a barn. Go over a stile to a field. Veer right down to a stile in the fence, cross and continue on to a wooded area. Go through a gate, across a track and over a stile into a field. Continue ahead, over another stile and up a bank, crossing a track (with a footpath signpost) to reach yet another stile. Proceed on to the next stile in the facing fence and then go to the top left

76

corner of the field. Cross a stile to a road, and turn right. Go up the hill, past Foxborough and through a wicket gate on the left to get on to **Dover's Hill** (see Walk 8). Continue right, between two seats, and then go right to the car park. Pass through to the road and turn left, following the Cotswold Way – arrows with white dots – from here. Proceed to a crossroads. Turn right and use a path beside a field on the left. Go over a stone stile, turn left and go through a gap in a stone wall right. Following the Cotswold Way, go along 'The Mile Drive', where horse racing took place in the 18th century. Continue across fields and Buckle Street to the Fish Hill picnic area. Cross the A44 to the Fish Inn. Pass to the right of the Fish Motor Company and enter a wood – still following the Cotswold Way – and, on emerging, go up a field and make for **Broadway Tower**.

From the tower, in Broadway Country Park, follow the Cotswold Way downhill to reach the A44 in Broadway. On reaching the road, turn left down the main street at the bottom of which you will find the Swan Inn, on the right. Go round the car park and to the right you will find Walnut Close, a cul de sac. At the end of the Close go right past a 'No entry' sign. This is the start of the Broadway-Willersey path. Pass a thatched cottage and go left in front of a red-brick factory. At the far end go through a wicket gate and on to a track between hawthorn hedges. In 200 yards go over a stile on the right and, keeping the same direction, pass behind some houses. At the end of the estate go over a footbridge into a field and walk round clockwise to the opposite side. Follow the yellow arrows (either side of the hedge is OK) and continue ahead across two fields. Now move to the left of the hedge and go straight on across the fields to arrive at the side of the old railway. Follow this for two fields and then enter a wooded area. On emerging, turn right, away from the railway, towards a barn. Pass the barn and continue along the edge of the field to bungalows. Go left on to a path by electric poles and into a road on a housing estate. Turn right and keep right of the sign 'Hays Close' up to a T-junction of paths. Turn left and, passing Willersey School, return to the start.

POINTS OF INTEREST:
Willersey – A Cotswold village, complete with duck pond, and many old buildings.
Broadway Tower – Constructed in about 1800 by the Earl of Coventry. It is about 55 feet high and there are magnificent views from the top.
Broadway – An old coaching village where extra horses were provided to get up Fish Hill. Now busy with tourists, it has many antique shops and art galleries.

REFRESHMENTS:
The Bell Inn, Willersey (tel no: 0386 852350)
Numerous places in Broadway.

Walk 34 CLEEVE CLOUD AND WEST DOWN 9m (14.5km)

Maps: OS Sheets Landranger 163; Pathfinder SP 02/12.

A moderately easy walk with superb views. Some mud after heavy rain, but it dries out well.

Start: At 989272, in the quarry near Cleeve Hill Golf Club.

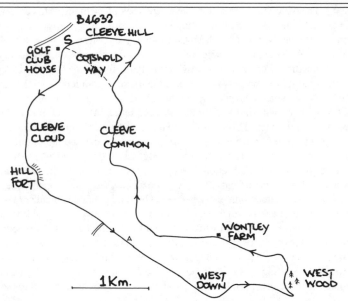

Return to the cattle grid (note that meals and/or refreshments are available at the adjacent clubhouse), and turn left uphill on a well-defined track. In about 200 yards turn right behind iron railings around a disused quarry and walk towards the high ground in front, keeping the fairway on your left. At the top, **Cleeve Cloud**, seek out the topograph from which many places of interest in the vale below and beyond can be identified. Walk southerly, along the edge of the escarpment, keeping the links on your left while enjoying the magnificent views on your right. The path takes you through an **Iron Age hill fort**, now encircling the thirteenth green, and then past two small clumps of trees on your left. There you turn your back on the vale, going half-left towards the wireless masts in view on the horizon. In limited visibility follow a track parallel to the dry-stone wall on your right.

Leave the masts on your right and continue on in the same direction along the sheep walk known as West Down. It is here that you may encounter mud but it is easily avoided. Go under power cables, through a gate in a fence, and follow a track through gorse on the left to a gate and cattle grid. Go through the gate and turn right down a well-defined track to a deteriorating metalled road in a secluded valley. Turn left, passing Westwood House on the right, through a field gate, and bear half-left on paths along a grassy bottom, by-passing Wontley Farm. Ignore the track crossing at right-angles, and pass under power cables again to a gate giving access to Cleeve Common. Here, bear half-right again through the gorse. The route you should now follow is marked by posts bearing a yellow arrow and a white dot – the Cotswold Way. At first the path is fairly level, but it shortly descends steeply to a narrow valley, where it turns right and soon passes the source of the River Isbourne. Within about 300 yards the infant river is dammed, and here you bear left along the foot of the hill until you arrive at a point where a dry-stone wall around a small wood on your right touches the path. The direct route back to the car park is by following the Cotswold Way straight up the steep hill in front. This last effort may be pleasantly avoided by turning right-handed around the wood, following the track alongside the wall, bearing left up a short bank where it divides, and passing through two gates on to the hill again. The car park is now straight ahead.

POINTS OF INTEREST:

Cleeve Cloud – 1040 feet high. Not quite the highest point of the Cotswolds but the one with the best views. The Malverns dominate the vale below but look for The Lickeys near Birmingham, May Hill beyond Gloucester, the Sugar Loaf near Abergavenny and the Black Mountains of Wales.

Iron Age hill fort – An almost complete double ring of raised mounds, breached only where the golf link enters. Note the superb defensive position selected, but spare a thought to the garrison in those far-off cold winters.

REFRESHMENTS:

Cleeve Hill Golf Club (tel no: 024267 2025).

WOLD VILLAGES 10m (16km)
Map: OS Sheets Landranger 163; Pathfinder SP 01/11.
A ramble in the true Cotswold countryside.
Start: At 104208, the car park in Notgrove.

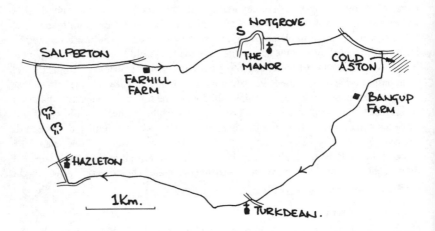

Turn right from the car park and follow the road. Take the first right turn down the back of the church. Where the road bends towards the church go through a field gate on the left. Go up the bank in the field to the top right and a gate leading on to a track. Turn right. Go along to the row of beech trees on the left and enter this avenue through a gate. Proceed to the far end and the road to **Cold Aston**. Turn right on the road and after ¼ mile look for a road right marked 'Unsuitable for Motors'. If you would like refreshment at this point the Plough Inn is 400 yards on, on the right. Continue your walk down the 'Unsuitable' road towards Turkdean. It deteriorates into a track after Bangup Farm but there is no problem in following it for nearly 2 miles. As you go up a slope into **Turkdean** keep right by the triangular green and cross the road to the farm buildings. Go to the far end of these and turn left down a farm track to a red gate in front of a yard. Cross this to another red gate and go into a field. Now follow the track towards

Hazleton. After about $^1/_2$ mile, where the valley forks, keep left towards a fir wood. Continue up past Hill Bern and into **Hazleton**.

The track now becomes a road. Go up past the first cottages to turn right by Plum Tree Cottage. Proceed forward to the church and at the crossroads nearby go straight across on to a farm track. Continue up to a farm and your path is now straight ahead at the side of a wood. At the end of the wood pass through a gate and continue through two fields with a wall on your left to a gate leading to an avenue of trees. Pass through to the road. (Salperton Park House and church are down to your left here. This is a great show of aconites and snowdrops in late winter.)

Proceed now to the right on to a road and continue for about $^1/_2$ mile down to Farhill Farm. Go right of the buildings down a rough track to a gateway and straight on down the field, keeping in the valley. Recently this path was not clear, but as a guide, make for the gate in the bottom facing hedge. Pass through this and turn right towards a fence and then left up to a gate and on to a second gate by a barn. Here a road begins which takes you to the top of the rise. In front are Notgrove Manor gates, complete with mermaid. Turn left here. Go along to a cricket field, then turn right down to the end of the field, then turn left and back to **Notgrove** and the car park.

POINTS OF INTEREST:
Cold Aston – Now named 'Aston Blank' to distinguish it from Cold Ashton near Bath. Some nice old houses and again a church of Norman origin.
Turkdean – A village of two halves: up the hill and down the hill. There are nice flowers here in the spring.
Hazleton – Another old church alongside farm buildings: a stone coffin lies outside. Much restoration of older farm buildings is going on.
Notgrove – According to an old rhyme it derives its name from nearby nut groves. The church, of Norman origin,has several interesting features as has the manor house with its trimmed yew trees.

REFRESHMENTS:
The Plough Inn, Cold Aston (tel no: 0451 21459).

Walk 36   ROBINSWOOD HILL COUNTRY PARK   4m (6.5km)

Maps: OS Sheets Landranger 162; Pathfinder SO 81/91.

A pleasant walk near Gloucester in a designated Country Park.

Start: The car park at Robinswood Hill Country Park.

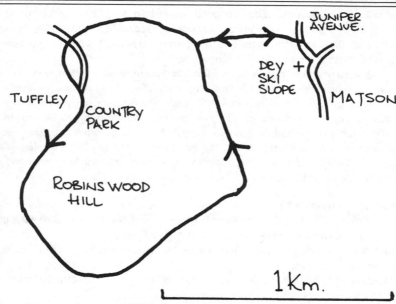

From the car park go to the right of the **Country Park** Information Centre and immediately take the right fork on to a track leading towards a large oak tree. Go straight over the crossing track, and to the left of the tree on a wide green path. Take two right forks in quick succession and continue up the steep bank in front of you. At the top of the climb, and just before you reach the scrub, turn left on a footpath to join a gritted track at a fork. Here turn sharp right, ignoring the track going uphill, and continue on the one which runs fairly level following the contour lines around the hill, keeping the higher ground on your left, and declining all side tracks. (For the purposes of this walk it is better to disregard the profusion of waymark posts.) The track will shortly take you along the top edge of a conifer plantation on your right, and on to fairly open ground where there is a convergence of several tracks. Go straight ahead at this junction through some light scrub on to more open ground which offers you a panoramic view of the city of Gloucester. Follow the main track, which lines up with the city gas-holder, downhill to the edge of a wood, where it turns left and then right to enter a wood. Here the descent becomes very steep and, in wet weather, slippery, but you are assisted by steps to the level ground below. At the T-junction, if you wish to go to the dry ski slope, turn right on the concrete track and, where it turns sharp left, go straight ahead through the woodland, across a field to join a road, Juniper Avenue,behind houses on an estate. Turn right and right again into Matson Lane, pass between **St Katherine's Church** on the right and **Selwyn School** on the left and the ski slope is on your right. After your visit, retrace your steps to where you finished your descent and joined the concrete track, and continue straight on with houses on your right. In a hundred yards or so you will see the car park from where you started.

POINTS OF INTEREST:
Robinswood Hill Country Park – A designated Country Park close to the city of Gloucester. The dry ski slope, open all year round, offers tuition to all standards of skier. The Information Centre is open Thursday to Sunday, office hours.
St Katherine's Church – A fine 18th-century church.
Selwyn School – Note the large sundial on the south wall.

REFRESHMENTS:
Gloucester Ski Centre, Matson Lane, Gloucester (tel no: 0452 414300).

Walk 37   SEVERN WAY PATH $4^1/_2$ m (7km)

Maps: OS Sheets Landranger 162; Pathfinder SO 82/92.

A combined hill-top and riverside walk.

Start: The Red Lion Inn at Wainlode.

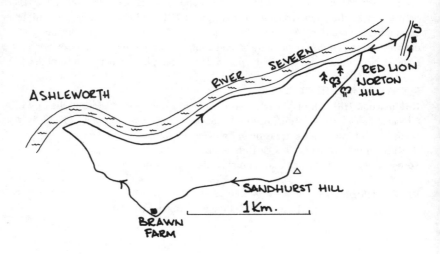

From the inn, cross left to the orchard and go over a stile on to the **Severn Way Path** (look for the green sign with a ship). Continue through an orchard and over another stile at the top of the bank. Turning right, follow the fence with views down to the river, and at the corner of the field cross a stile and start to ascend. Leave the Severn Way here (do not enter the wood). Climb, instead, up the field with the wood on your right, following yellow waymarks. Cross another stile and climb to the top of the hill. Continue ahead, join a track and proceed to where trees meet from left and right. Pass through a gate and go straight ahead across a field. The track all the time gets firmer the farther you go. At the far end of the field an Ordnance Survey pillar will be seen – a good vantage point. Continue on the track and descend towards Sandhurst. Pass some farm buildings on the right and descend through a gate on to a minor road – this is Brawn Farm. Turn right on to the road in front of a white house. This road starts with a good surface but it deteriorates quite quickly and is only a track by the time you get to the River Severn after about $\frac{1}{2}$ mile.

The riverside pub at Ashleworth is across the river. However, we rejoin the Severn Way Path which will be followed back to **Wainlode**. There is a stile, right, to gain access to a field. Follow a path, on the riverside, across four fields for about 1 mile, then cross a stile into a wood and follow the well-used path. At one point in the wood ascend many steps to arrive at the bottom of a field. Follow the field round left, following arrows, to enter a wood and after 250 yards cross a stile into a field and return to the Red Lion on the same path you used at the start of the ramble.

POINTS OF INTEREST:

The Severn Way Path – The path goes from Tewkesbury to Shepperdine, and was opened on Easter Monday 1989 as part of the 100th anniversary year celebrations of Gloucestershire County Council. Over £40,000 was spent on preparing the path making footbridges, stiles and so on.

Wainlode – Wainlode Cliff just downstream from the Red Lion, is worth visiting.

REFRESHMENTS:

The Red Lion, Wainlode (tel no: 0452 730251).

Walk 38 PRINKNASH ABBEY AND PAINSWICK HILL $4\frac{1}{2}$ m (7km)
Maps: OS Sheets Landranger 162; Pathfinder SO 81/91.

A circular route round Prinknash Abbey and the neighbouring hills with glorious views over the Severn Valley.

Start: The Royal William pub near Cranham.

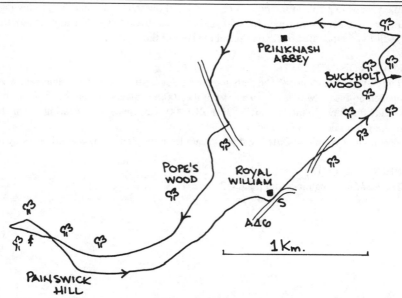

Walk on the left side of the A46 towards Cheltenham down to Cranham Corner. Cross over and turn right on to the road marked 'Cranham 1, Birdlip 3'. Just past 'Rough Park Bungalow' on the left enter Buckholt Wood and follow the Cotswold Way arrowheads (yellow arrows with white dots). It is here marked 'Coopers Hill 2.5km'. Your path joins a track which you now follow to the top of the hill. At the top follow a wall on the left and descend the steep slope. Where the track bends right, away from the wall, follow it round to cross-tracks with a rough island in the middle. Leave the Cotswold Way at this point, keeping left and descend to the main road (A46). To your right on the main road is a lay-by with a toilet. Continuing the walk, turn left and go up to the bend in the road. It is best to walk on the right-hand side of road here, but be very careful. Right on the bend opposite a cottage, descend to a gap in the wall and go through an overgrown area and over a stile in the gate. Go down the field and over a stile, making towards chestnut trees. There are good views of **Prinknash Abbey** and its grounds to the left.

Having gone over a stile by the trees, go forward and at the brow of the hill go down a cultivated field aiming for the far left corner. There is usually a well-used path to follow. The Gloucester dry ski slope can be seen here to the far right. Arriving at the corner – which could be muddy – pass over a stile into a wooded area, over a footbridge and cross the field to the estate road. You could possibly see the Prinknash abbey deer up the road to the left.

Continue over the road and cross a stile. Following a hedge/fence on your left, ascend the field. In 250 yards cross a stile into the next field, turn right and go along to the road. Turn left up the road and, passing St Peter's Grange, enter the wood on the right. It is marked Pope's Wood and you follow the bridleway. In 120 yards, at an open space with several tracks leading off, carry straight ahead following blue arrows. After $^1/_2$ mile (at about the half-way point), still in the wood, turn right at a T-junction where there is a Pope's Wood notice. Continue ahead, still in wood but now with the fields right. Go on round to the Gloucester-Painswick road. Turn left on the road and in 400 yards take the first track left on to **Painswick Hill**.

Just keep straight ahead on the main track, climbing gradually. Continue up past a bungalow and emerge on to golf links. There is a water tank in the wood to the left. At this point, if you wish to climb to the highest point – Painswick Beacon – turn right and in a few yards you will see the marker about 300 yards ahead. Return to the main track and continue ahead, following a wood left. Gradually the track improves into a road which you follow down to the Royal William.

POINTS OF INTEREST:
Prinknash Abbey – Well worth a visit, about $^1/_2$ mile down the A46 towards Cheltenham from the Royal William.
Painswick Hill – The site of the Iron Age Fort of Kimsbury. The highest point, the Beacon, is nearly 300 metres high.

REFRESHMENTS:
The Royal William, Cranham (tel no: 0452 813650).
Prinknash Abbey, *tea shop* (tel no: 0452 812455).

Walk 39   DEERHURST TO APPERLEY   5m (8km)

Maps: OS Sheets Landranger 150; Pathfinder SO 82/92.

A walk along the river bank, best in summer. A working vineyard is nearby.

Start: At 871297, St Mary's Church, Deerhurst.

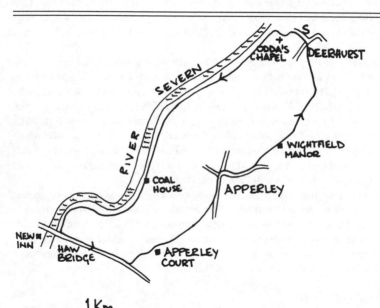

Consider visiting **St Mary's** and **Odda's Chapel** before setting off. Both are well signposted. From the chapel go through the gate opposite, follow the footpath to the river bank and turn left along the raised river defences, signposted as the Severn Way (see Walk 37), for about 1½ miles until you arrive at The Coal House Inn, Apperley; this is a pleasant setting in which to stop for refreshment. Just beyond the pub look for the footpath across the caravan site, and continue along the river bank until you reach Haw Bridge. There is a public house at the other end of Haw Bridge providing food and a place to eat outside if you wish. Otherwise, turn left along the busy road for about 1,200 yards and go through a white gate on your left immediately opposite a lane coming in from your right. The footpath climbs through a delightful wood which is carpeted with spring flowers in season. This Right of Way passes through the grounds of Apperley Court, to the left of the house, and straight on down the drive which becomes a lane leading to Apperley.

After passing the church, merge with another lane near the War Memorial, and continue to a crossroads where there is the village shop and post office on the left. Here turn sharp right. Immediately before the village hall turn left on to a footpath across the sports ground, cross the footbridge and turn half-right making for a track running beside some trees behind Wightfield Manor. Turn left on the track, and pass into the next field to go straight ahead keeping the hedge on your right. The clear path takes you across one more field to a point just in front of an old red-brick house, The Vicarage, where three large metal farm gates cannot be missed. Here turn left into the lane passing Abbot's Court Farm, turn right at the T-junction and back to your car.

POINTS OF INTEREST:
St Mary's Church – Important Saxon church with claims to being the oldest and largest of its type in England. Dated from 700 AD.
Odda's Chapel – Dated 1056 AD.
Apperley – Tapestry Wines Ltd, The Vineyard, Wells Farm, Apperley (tel no: 045278 435). Open 1 May - 30 September. Ring for times. Located off walk on the B4213.

REFRESHMENTS:
The Coal House Inn, Apperley (tel no: 045278 211).
The New Inn, Haw Bridge (tel no: 045278 275).

Walks 40 and 41 **FLAXLEY WOODS AND WELSHBURY** 5m (8km)
or 5^1/$_2$m (8.5km)
Maps: OS Sheets Landranger 162; Outdoor Leisure 14.
A pleasant walk partly through woodland, partly through fields.
Start: At 693152, in the lane ^{1}/$_4$ mile east of Flaxley Church.

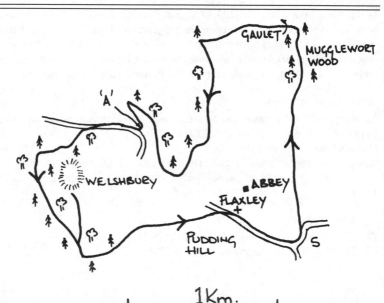

From the start a footpath heads north. After a few yards, climb a flight of steps to the
right then cross a stile to enter a field. Follow the nearer fence, climbing gradually and
passing two field boundaries, the first by means of a stile. When level ground is reached
climb over another stile to enter Mugglewort Wood. The path is well defined as it
descends gradually through broad-leafed trees with dense conifers to the left. It
emerges on to a broad track which you should follow to the right for about 70 yards.
Look out for a narrow path leading down to the left. This is steep and can be slippery
when wet, but in a short time a footbridge is reached. Cross the bridge and immediately
turn left making for an obvious gap in a line of trees and bushes. Climb steeply through
the bracken above and on over the grassy shoulder ahead. Over the brow the Gaulet
Farm can be seen below, and you should make for a gate on the nearer fence, to the right

of the buildings. Through the gate, go diagonally to the left up through the farmyard, then horizontally, keeping the uppermost shed on the right. Pass through two gates in quick succession then go slightly right to follow a line of trees marking the course of a small stream. (It may be an advantage at one point to cross the watercourse and progress up the field on the right.)

Make for the corner of the masses of woodland that now converge. A stile will be found near the corner and although the path beyond may appear to be overgrown, persevere, for in 10 yards there is a comfortably wide track. Go left and follow this track for about 1 mile as it describes a U-shaped course near the periphery of Flaxley Woods. Where three tracks in close succession come in from the right, look for a crossing of the fence to the left. There is no stile here, although this is a right of way, but the wire fence is easily negotiated. Go oblique left through a gap between bushes and make for a footbridge over the valley brook. The way up to the public road is now obvious. (*)

Turn right along the road for $^1/_4$ mile. Almost opposite a corrugated shed a path leads up obliquely on the left. This path, muddy when wet, soon passes through a gate, gradually increasing its distance from the road as it gains height. Emerging into a clearing, turn left on a broad grassy way that gives pleasant walking. With woodland to the left, the views to the right gradually open up as height is increased. The path levels off as it veers leftward. At a junction, where a gate on the right is an exit from the wood, a path leads upwards to the left. This reaches the hill-top earthworks of **Welshbury** after about $^1/_4$ mile – an interesting diversion. If you visit the hilltop, return back down the same path, then turn your attention to the gate. It may be padlocked but there is a small stile on its left. Turn immediately left and hug the perimeter of the wood. You will pass about half a dozen fences in fairly quick succession. The first is a rather broken-down affair that can be stepped over, and the second is low down to the left in a grassy ditch. The rest are straightforward, if somewhat awkward. After the last one keep on in the same line across the flank of Pudding Hill. Soon you will see the spire of Flaxley Church and you can use this as a marker. Aim towards the bottom corner of the field where a stile gives access to the next field. A few yards away another stile takes you to a flight of diminutive steps, thoughtfully provided to lead you down to the road almost opposite the church. Go right along the road back to the starting point.

POINTS OF INTEREST:
Welshbury – The earthworks of a prehistoric camp of undetermined date. Although overgrown by trees, lines of ditch and dike can still be made out.
(*) See Walk 42

Maps: OS Sheets Landranger 162; Outdoor Leisure 14.
A walk partly through woodland, partly through fields.
Start: At 693152, in the lane $^1/_4$ mile east of Flaxley Church.

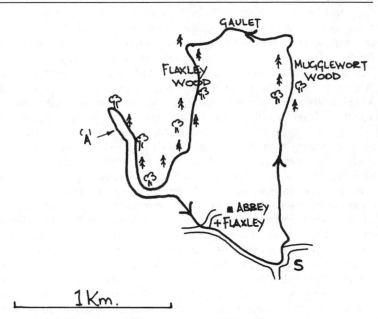

This walk is as for Walks 40 and 41 as far as the point marked (*).

Do not emerge into the road but walk left towards the reddish-coloured house. Near the garden gate cross a stile on the right and head across the field to a gate in the fence opposite. Now walk round the perimeter of the woodland passing two more fences (gates) and at one point re-crossing the brook. At a point where the edge of the woodland veers away on the other side of the fence, turn half-right and make for the spire of Flaxley Church. On the way you will cross the brook again by means of a footbridge. The exit is on to the opening of **Flaxley Abbey** drive where the fence can easily be stepped over – at present there is no stile, but this is a Right of Way.

POINTS OF INTEREST:
Flaxley Abbey – A moated house built on the site of a former Cistercian Abbey and including parts of the original building. The refectory (c.1148) and abbots' hall (c.1350) have been preserved. Sadly the abbey is not open to the public.

Walk 43　　**MAY HILL TO CLIFFORDS MESNE**　　5 m (8km)

Maps: OS Sheets Landranger 162; Pathfinder SO 62/72.

Pleasant walking near one of Gloucestershire's landmarks.

Start: At 692223, in the lane ¹/₂ mile from the Yew Tree Inn, Clifford Mesne.

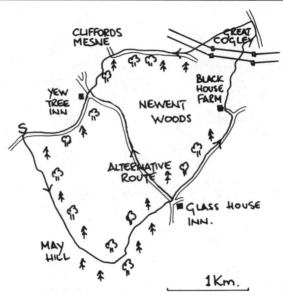

On the opposite side of the lane a gate opens on to a track. Follow this until the track levels off, where there is a stone wall. Swing left and follow the wall until a gate gives access to **May Hill.** Make straight for the distinctive clump of trees seen on the summit. Keep on over the summit in the same line and as you begin to descend you will find yourself between two masses of forestry that gradually converge. Cross a stile and later take a left branch that goes past an unusually shaped house. At a T-junction go left to a large gate 30 yards away. On the other side of the gate a path goes right, down through woodland. In little over ¹/₂ mile a stile is crossed to a public road. You can now return to the starting point by turning left and walking along the lane through Newent Woods, towards Cliffords Mesne, turning left just before entering the village to climb the hill past the Yew Tree Inn.

94

Otherwise, you can take a longer route involving field as well as road walking. This way involves crossing a barbed wire fence where there is at present no stile or gate, although it is a public Right of Way.

Turn right for a few yards to a road junction where you go left, signed 'Newent'. After about $^3/_4$ mile turn left up a surfaced lane, signposted 'Blackhouse Farm'. Just before the farm buildings turn right to enter a field through a gate. Follow the track down, and after another gate climb the opposite slope keeping near to the left-hand boundary. After passing a shed look across the shallow valley in front. On the opposite slope, and slightly to the right, the corner of a fence features prominently: make straight for this. There is no stile or gate here, but the fence may be crossed, using a tree as an aid. Having done this go across the bottom of the next field to a stile, then cross the further field at an angle to the opposite side and walk along to a corner gate. Cross the next field to a stile to the right of an electricity pylon. Beyond this follow the field boundary down to a public road, then go left for 200 yards. After crossing a stream go left through a gate and straight across to a second gate at its far end. From here three pylons are in the walker's field of view. Aim for the furthest right (and furthest away) and pass to the right of it. Go down and further right to a gate near the field's corner and beyond this through a small copse. Now keep to the right-hand boundary as you climb the opposing slope. When you reach a small artificial lake keep to its left shore to reach a track. Turn right and follow this out to the public road.

Walk along the road in the same direction, with woodland to the left. As the houses of Cliffords Mesne begin to appear, where the main lane swings right, bear left and after 120 yards turn left. Where this lane bends left, go straight ahead, through a gate into a field. Keep to the right-hand edge and at the far end go along a path, stepping over a low stile. Emerging on to another path, bear left over a footbridge and go to a road. Go straight across and up the lane opposite, past the Yew Tree Inn. Follow the lane back to the car park.

POINTS OF INTEREST:

May Hill – A fine viewpoint with views in all directions. The Black Mountains can be seen to the west, Malverns to the north and Cotswolds to the south-west. Legend has it that there are 99 trees in the summit clump.

REFRESHMENTS:

Yew Tree Inn, Cliffords Mesne (tel no: 0531 820719). Bar meals.
The Glass House Inn, Glasshouse Hill (tel no: 0452 830529). Bar meals daily except Sunday.

Walk 44   AROUND ASHLEWORTH   6¹/₂m (10km)

Maps: OS Sheets Landranger 162; Pathfinder SO 82/92.

A walk through fields and along the River Severn.

Start: At 819251, near the Boat Inn, Ashleworth. On the early part of the walk look for yellow arrow waymarkers.

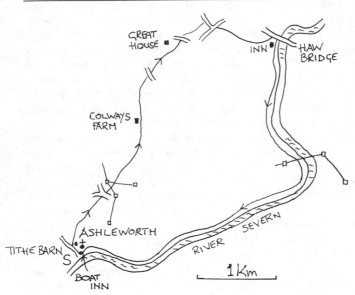

Go up the lane, away from **Ashleworth** and the river. Go round the right-hand bend, with Ashleworth Court to the right. Where the lane bends left, keep straight on following the field boundary, a line of poplars. Keep in the same field where the boundary kinks (ignore two stiles to the left) and continue to the end of the field. Go over a stile and maintain the same line to the corner of the next field where there is access to a road. Cross the road and a little to the left a gate gives access to a field. Aim slightly left of an electricity pylon, and cross the field to a stile. Now aim slightly left of a corrugated iron barn across the next field. A gate will be found and the walker must now bear slightly left to a footbridge that is a little to the right of a shattered tree on the opposite side of the next field. The footbridge has a 'Vee' stile at each end and beyond it an upright stile has to be surmounted. About 100 yards away a junction of hedges is it an upright stile has to be surmounted. About 100 yards away a junction of hedges is the next point to aim for. Here there are two more 'Vee' stiles with a plank bridge between. At the end of the next field three trees can be seen. Cross the stile just to the left of them.

The way is now along the right-hand field boundary towards Colways Farm and bungalow. Before reaching the buildings, go right through a waymarked gate. Bear left to go to the right of a barn. Cross the farm access road and bear right, as waymarked, to follow a fence. Follow the fence, it is on your left, around left and right bends to reach a stile in a corner. Go over and bear right along a stony track. Go through a gate and follow the track to a stile on to a road. Across the road a wicket gate leads to a small orchard with a stile on the other side. A distant house with prominent half timbering can be used as a marker in crossing the next two fields, the first to a stile, the second to a gate. Now aim to the right of the house and cross the next field diagonally to a stile. A further stile a few yards away and some steps lead down to another road.

On entering the field on the other side bear right diagonally to a gate and beyond cross a stream and rather upright stile (not waymarked). Now bear left to a gate and access to a public road. Turn right, walk down the road to a T-junction, and keep on in the same line. Cross two stiles to the left of a large gate and walk down the left-hand field boundary. After negotiating a footbridge and another stile, cross a further field in the same line. After crossing two more stiles aim for a gate at the far end of a wire fence a few yards to the left. Beyond this, keep adjacent to the right-hand field boundary to emerge on a lane a few yards from Haw Bridge. The New Inn is here. A metal gate that doubles as a 'Vee' stile gives access to a good path but this comes to an end after a short distance to be replaced by a grassy walk for the Boat Inn and the start.

POINTS OF INTEREST:
Ashleworth – The 15th-century tithe barn now belongs to the National Trust. It is open daily from 25 March to 31 October.

REFRESHMENTS:
The Boat Inn, Ashleworth (tel no: 045270 272).
The New Inn, Haw Bridge (tel no: 045278 275).

Walk 45   FROM AVON TO SEVERN   7¹/₂m (12km)

Maps: OS Sheets Landranger 150; Pathfinder SO 83/93.

A level walk, along the banks of two fine rivers.

Start:At 894333, King John's Bridge, Tewkesbury.

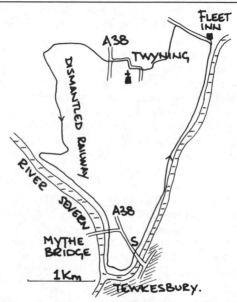

Cross the stile on the north-western side of the King John's Bridge, **Tewkesbury**, pass under the railway arch and follow the footpath along the bank of the River Avon to **Twyning.** Turn left by the side of The Fleet Inn and, within a few yards, the Village Inn (both good places to eat), and just beyond the village stores turn left on to a signposted track by the side of a house named Maryville. The track leads to a field; keep the poplar trees on your left looking out for a waymark sign on one of them about two-thirds of the way along, then bear half-right across the field towards Twyning Church. At the pond skirt right to avoid mud, go over the stile in the corner, then straight ahead leaving the church on your left.

At the T-junction turn right, then first left to cross the A38 to the footpath opposite the junction. Cross the field diagonally, going between two large trees and to the right of a small enclosure towards red-brick buildings. Go around the back of Gardeners

Cottage in a U-manoeuvre, then go through a farm gate and turn right, keeping close to the fence on the right. When it turns right continue straight ahead, crossing the fence where necessary, to emerge into a lane by a white house next to an old red-brick barn. Turn left, and left again through a farm gate just past the dismantled railway track, to walk through meadowland. In the first field the path is parallel to the hedge on the left: in the next steer a straight course slightly to the left of two large trees in the middle of the field to finish up with a hedge on your right and pass through the gate ahead.

After the next gate go slightly left and downhill on a wide track to a junction of several tracks and follow the lane marked as a footpath, passing a caravan site on the left, and go over a stile into a field. Go about 25 yards, then turn at right-angles towards a gate in the hedge to follow a footpath to the banks of the River Severn. Here turn left and follow the river to the Mythe Bridge, a white-painted cast-iron structure, where you pass between a garden and the river, through one of the smaller arches of the bridge. Go across the manicured banks fronting the water works, keeping to the right of the large pumphouse. The footpath then follows the course of the Severn to its confluence with the Old Avon, and via this river bank back to King John's Bridge.

POINTS OF INTEREST:

Tewkesbury – A fine, historic city with a magnificent abbey.
Twyning – Be sure to visit the church of St Mary Magdalene.
Mythe Bridge – King John's Castle, and Mythe Tut, or Royal Hill, nearby have a Saxon history.

REFRESHMENTS:

The Fleet Inn, Twyning (tel no: 0684 292561).
The Village Inn, Twyning (tel no: 0684 293500).
There are several ancient pubs and a wide variety of eating places in Tewkesbury.

NORTH WEST DEAN FOREST $7\frac{1}{2}$m (12km)
Maps: OS Sheets Landranger 162; Outdoor Leisure 14.
An undulating walk through mixed forestry.
Start: At 624124, the Forestry Commission site near Speech
House. The walk is waymarked with yellow arrows.

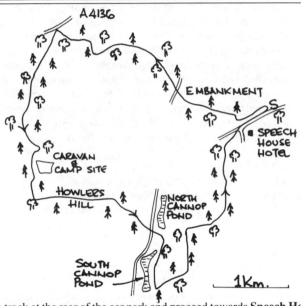

Take the track at the rear of the car park and proceed towards **Speech House** until you are level with the hotel. Cross the stile on the right, go down a slope and turn left along a well-defined track. As you leave the trees the 'Giant Chair', an item on the Forestry Commission's Sculpture Trail, can be seen ahead. Keep on past the structure and stay on the main track, bearing right, and ignoring all junctions. Eventually a dismantled railway on an embankment (stile on one side) is crossed and the B4234 can be seen ahead. Cross the road and go ahead, crossing several junctions. Continue up the steep slope and over the brow of the hill, then turn right at the next junction and follow the broad track until it reaches the A4136 where there is a signpost of footpaths. Turn left in the direction of Mile End following yellow arrows. The route gradually edges away from the main road on the right. Where a cross-track is encountered, the continuation is slightly to the right – the yellow arrows are hard to see, but the path is just discernible. Eventually you come to a broad forestry road: cross it and continue in the same line. There has been much tree felling here and arrows are few and far between, but soon you will begin to converge on a main forestry road to your left. When you reach it, bear right along it. Keep to this broad way as it gradually veers left and stay with it until a line of power cables is encountered. Now turn sharply right and walk on a course parallel with the cables. To your left the caravan site at Worcester Lodge will come into view and when you reach the corner of the site turn left to follow its western boundary.

Keep in the same line through further woodland to emerge on a road. Turn right. The road veers left and will soon join the B4226 near the Howlers Hill landfill site. Cross the road and go straight into the trees. After little more than 100 yards, turn left. Crossing another track, go on for $^1/_4$ mile and take a not too obvious narrow path to the left . This path descends through dense forest (in places you really have to look hard for the arrows) and eventually reaches the B4234. Cross the road and keep straight on. You are now between the two Cannop Ponds. Cross the northern pond's outlet and turn right through the picnic site. The eastern shore of the southern pond is now followed to the south-east corner where you move left on to the main track, a dismantled railway, and look for a junction where two tracks come in from the east. Take the more northerly of these by crossing the stile. After about $^1/_4$ mile turn left and after another 600 yards turn right up the hill. After a similar distance go left and after $^1/_4$ mile bear left again. You are nearing the B4226 but after a stile turn right and keep fairly parallel to the road until Speech House is reached. You can return to the car park either along the road, or by going down by the obelisk and over a stile to go right along the footpath.

POINTS OF INTEREST:

Speech House – Now an hotel, this was built as a court house, about 1680, where the foresters could settle their disputes. The Forest Court is still held here, ten times a year.

REFRESHMENTS:
Speech House Hotel (tel no: 0594 22607).

Walk 47   **KEMPLEY AND DYMOCK**   8m (13km)

Maps: OS Sheets Landranger 149; Pathfinder SO 62/72 & 63/73.
*A walk through meadow and woodland, especially attractive
when the wild daffodils are in bloom.*
Start: At 678284, the car park at Queens Wood.

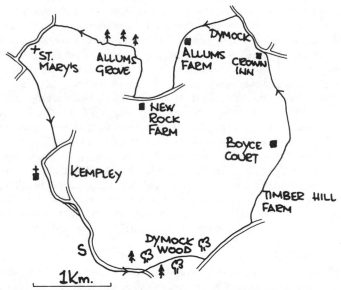

The walk is partially waymarked with a yellow arrow and black dot. Turn right from
the car park on to the road for about 350 yards and, when woodland recommences on
your left, go left on to the first drive. Follow this track for about 100 yards until it starts
to descend, then turn right on a waymarked track to a minor road. Turn right and,
immediately before the motorway bridge, turn left with the motorway on your right.
When the lane winds to the left, go straight ahead through a gate to the end of the third
field where you go left along the brook to a stile. Cross the track, go ahead over two
fields to skirt around Timber Hill Farm on your right, and rejoin the track the other side
of the farm. Go left through two fields, over a cattle grid, and turn right over a bridge
and then immediately left. Pass between two brick pillars at Boyce Court, and turn right
over the canal bridge and left over the stile to follow the disused canal. Pass over a

102

footbridge and walk with the hedge and brook on your right until they swing sharply away to the right. Go ahead steering for Dymock church, traversing four fields, one of which contains an orchard, to emerge on a road opposite the Beauchamp Arms. Turn left to pass the Crown Inn and walk on the B4125 road through **Dymock**.

At the top of the rise, just a few yards beyond the speed signs, turn left on to a track leading to Allums Farm. Where the track bears left down to the farm go ahead with the hedge on your right, then left around the corner of the outbuildings. Cross a field, passing to the right of the water trough. Go through a gate into an orchard and bear right to follow the left-hand hedge to the far end. Cross a stile and one more field to the road. Turn right, passing New Rock Farm on the left, and in about 200 yards go over the stile on your right and follow the boundary of Allums Grove for about 100 yards. Now veer half-right up the bank towards a footbridge and cross the brook. Go over a stile into the wood ahead and follow the path to another stile on your right taking you into the field again. Turn left for a few yards, re-enter the wood by another stile and stay on the main track to an iron gate. Keep to the left of the pond, turn right just past some ruins and cross a ditch into the next field. Keep the hedge on your left until it turns sharply away, then go across the corner of the field and over a stile. Proceed with the hedge on your right to pass between some tall trees, over **Kempley Brook** into the next field, and bear half-left across fields to join the road by a red-brick house. Go left, passing St Mary's Church, to a T-junction. Turn left. When the road swings right, enter the field by a farm and go straight on to a large tree in the far hedge. Pass through a gate and continue in the same direction keeping close to the hedge or brook on your left until you reach a road again. To visit St Edward's Church turn right at this point and then left. Afterwards, continue on the road through the village back to your car.

POINTS OF INTEREST:

Dymock – St Mary's Church, of Saxon/Norman origin, contains exhibitions of work of the Dymock Poets. The White House, birthplace of John Kyrle in 1637. This humanitarian was celebrated as *The Man of Ross* in Pope's *Moral Epistle*.

Kempley – St Mary's Church has 12th-century frescoes and wall paintings. St Edward's Church, from the 20th century, is described as a miniature cathedral dedicated to the Arts and Crafts Movement.

REFRESHMENTS:

The Crown Inn, Dymock (tel no: 053185 660).
The Beauchamp Arms, Dymock (tel no: 053185 266).

Walk 48   WESTBURY AND THE SEVERN'S BANK   8m (13km)

Maps: OS Sheets Landranger 162; Pathfinder SO 61/71.

A level walk, half of which is along the Severn bank.

Start: At 719139, a lay-by in front of the Court Garden, Westbury-on-Severn.

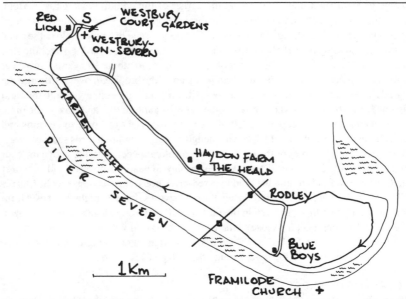

Walk westwards a short distance and turn left at the Red Lion into Bell Lane. Go past the **Westbury-on-Severn** church tower and steeple which is separated from the main church building. Turn left across the churchyard to an exit in the far corner. Cross a stile into a small field then, having crossed a stream by means of a bridge, go over another stile into a larger field. Bearing marginally left, aim for a gap in the fence on the opposite side and then in about the same line cross the next field to a footbridge. A galvanised gate about 50 yards away gives access to a lane where you go left. After 150 yards turn right at a T-junction and walk along this lane for about 2 miles, passing several farms. A little more than $^1/_2$ mile after passing underneath power cables, and immediately after a sharp right-hand bend, go left between Cider Mill Cottage and Dove House. Follow this track, stony at times, until after almost 1 mile you are confronted by three gates.

Go through the middle one and move left to gain the crest of the flood-retaining embankment and walk along it with the River Severn to your left.

Cross two stiles and then you will encounter a water flow control installation where there are two more stiles. On the opposite side of the river you can see the end of the old Stroudwater Canal and, a few yards further west, Framilode Church among trees. Soon Blue Boys Farm appears ahead and as you approach the path is diverted slightly right. Just before the buildings, a stile allows you to go left to rejoin the embankment, which forms the route for the next 2 miles.

Several fences are encountered, each one crossed by a stile except one, near an electricity pylon, where there is a gate. Where the land ahead begins to rise, bear right a little to a stile that gives access to a sloping field. For the next $\frac{1}{2}$ mile the route is close to the Garden Cliff, a sheer drop on the left to the river, and, although this is fenced, care should be exercised if you are accompanied by children or dogs. After three further stiles walk down the left-hand edge of field and turn right along the far boundary to a stile next to Cliff Cottage. Turn left along the lane, regaining the riverside and walk along a broad track to an inlet where a stream joins the Severn through a sluice. Walk round until opposite a house and having crossed the stream turn right through a small metal gate. Now follow the bank of the stream, negotiating a pair of stiles to reach another stile. Make for the church steeple and reach the end of Bell Lane. Walk back past the church to the main road and the start.

POINTS OF INTEREST:

Westbury-on-Severn – The Court Garden dates from about 1700 and is the earliest Dutch-style garden surviving in England. Built round water canals, the garden includes a quaint pavilion. The site now belongs to the National Trust. The 13th-century tower of the church is crowned by a steeple composed almost entirely of wood. The framework of oak is covered by timber shingles, the weather vane being 153 feet above the ground. The church itself, separated from the tower by about 50 feet, is a collection of bits and pieces from about 1300, through to the 16th century.

REFRESHMENTS:

The Red Lion Inn, Westbury-on-Severn (tel no: 045276 221). Bar meals and restaurant.

Walk 49   **HIGHMEADOW WOOD**   8¹/₂m (13.5km)

Maps: OS Sheets Landranger 162; Outdoor Leisure 14.

A mostly woodland walk, in the latter stages along the River Wye.

Start: At 564160, the Forestry Commission's car park.

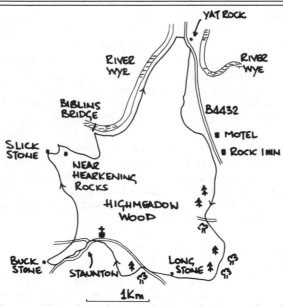

Go south on a wide track passing over the car park entrance. Bear left by a large oak and pass a cottage on the right. Go over a forestry road and about two miles from the start go across another road and along the side of Christchurch campsite. Go left on the south side of the campsite then right by a cottage. Cross a forestry road and take the path that leaves it at an angle. Two tracks come in from the right in quick succession: take the second, then at a junction go on in the same line on a broad forestry road. At a bend, bear left on a path. The path joins the A4136 and comes out by the **Long Stone.**

Go 40 yards along the road then cross to a path that leaves it at an angle. After about 200 yards join a forestry road and go slightly left. After 200 yards go right and shortly afterwards go right again on a green track. Follow this until it becomes stony and go to the main road almost opposite Staunton Church. The route goes left, just short of the main road, and follows a lane. Go left at the village shop. Follow the lane turning left at Bend Cottage and shortly go right through bracken, regaining the lane further up. Pass some houses and bear right to reach the **Buck Stone,** which is just over the brow.

Go right now and descend again towards Staunton. You will reach a metalled lane with the A4136 about 50 yards away. The White Horse is a short distance to the right. Go across to a narrow opening almost opposite and take the path down through the trees. At one point it becomes badly eroded and muddy, but it emerges on to a broad level track where you go right. After nearly $^1/_2$ mile you will suddenly see the **Suck Stone** up to the right. Go up the stepped path to it and pass up its right side, keeping on in the same line (steep in places). On reaching the overhanging bulk of the **Near Hearkening Rocks**, go left. At their end go right steeply round the rocks and keep in that line until the path emerges on to a broad forestry road. Go left for a few yards then right. At a T-junction go left but bear right at a fork. After another 60 yards cross a forestry track and keep on down. At one place go left, horizontally for 50 yards then continue the descent. It is steep now and care must be exercised especially when wet.

You will eventually reach a broad horizontal track beside the River Wye. **Biblins Bridge** is to the left but the route goes right. There are two tracks that follow the river bank: follow either, but after $^3/_4$ mile be sure you are on the right-hand one. This rises away from the other track and at its highest point fork right on a path that crosses the hillside at a comfortable gradient, with Symonds Yat now in view. Just below a barrier turn right on a waymarked, stepped path to arrive at the **Yat Rock** car park.

POINTS OF INTEREST:
The Long Stone – Believed to have been an ancient mustering point.
The Buck Stone –Near one of the highest points in the Forest of Dean, the spot commands fine views. The stone was originally a logan (rocking stone) but was displaced by vandals in 1885. Now cemented in its original position.
The Suck Stone – This is claimed to be the largest detached boulder in the country estimated to weigh between 4,000 and 14,000 tons.
The Near Hearkening Rocks – An overhanging mass of conglomerate, thought to have been used by gamekeepers listening for poachers.
Biblins Bridge – A suspension bridge for pedestrians only.
Yat Rock – Can be reached by a footpath that crosses the adjacent road by footbridge. Fine views up and down the River Wye.

REFRESHMENTS:
The refreshment hut in the car park is open from March to October.
The White Horse Inn, Staunton (tel no: 0594 33387). Bar meals available.

Walk 50 SYMONDS YAT ROCK TO CHRISTCHURCH 10m (16km)
Maps: OS Sheets Landranger 162; Outdoor Leisure 14.
Along the side of the River Wye and then through fine woodland.
Start: At 464160, the Forestry Commission's Yat Rock car park.

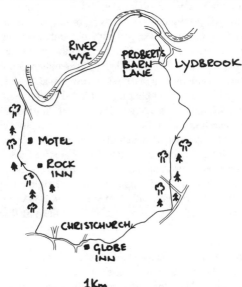

Start down the road, under the wooden footbridge, and turn right after 200 yards at some disused kilns, following 'Welsh Bicknor' on the finger post. The path meanders down through the trees, eventually joining a broad track at the bottom, where you bear right. This track now goes along the bank of the River Wye following the course of a former railway. After ¹/₂ mile a stile is encountered followed by two gates. Climb over the second. Shortly after a further stile, a sign directs you down steps to the left to another stile. Beyond a narrow path hugs the river bank. Where it passes a factory go under the former railway bridge and shortly after descend to cross a small footbridge. After crossing a stile a road will be seen to converge from the right. Another stile, by what appears to be a small pen, is crossed and 50 yards on a stile to the right gives access to the road. On the opposite side a footpath slants leftwards and upwards and then bends back to the right. At 'Radnors' cross a stile on the left. Almost immediately after

108

another stile an iron gate has to be crossed where you turn left along the field boundary. Go round right, crossing another stile to emerge in Probertsbarn Lane. Turn left down the lane which descends steeply to a sharp left-hand bend. A stile can be seen ahead surmounting a low bank. Cross the stile and turn half-right to go across a sloping field horizontally to the corner of a hedge. The route from now on is waymarked with yellow arrows but some of these are indistinct.

Follow the field boundary for a few yards, then bear right past an electricity pole to a stile. Go over and half-left to another corner that juts out and follow the field boundary. Cross a stile and carry on between fences, but turn right and quickly left at two junctions. The path eventually joins a metalled lane but after a short distance turn right up through bracken and bear left into the trees. Where the path intersects a levelled terrace (possibly an old tramway) which can be seen to go slightly left, keep straight on up the slope. Eventually the path joins a broad track along the edge of the forestry but after about 200 yards bear left through the trees. The path crosses a road and keeps on in line. When you come to a prominent forestry road go right for a few yards, then left along another forestry road.

The A4136 gradually converges from the left but keep on until the path meets the road (a finger post of walking routes can be seen on the other side). Do not cross the road but turn right on the path that leads out of the trees. Go straight up a metalled drive that can be seen ahead, and after a few yards, where it bends left, carry straight on along a path. When another metalled way is encountered, go straight on along it, but where that too bends left, carry straight on into forestry. A well-established footpath now takes you through pleasant woodland to emerge on a road. At a junction of roads go half-left, bisecting two roads. You will emerge on to a broader path that finishes at another road by a school. Carry on past the school and bear round right to a road junction where you turn left. Walk for about 100 yards (the Globe Inn is to the left) to a junction with the B4432. Turn right. In rather more than $^1/_2$ mile go straight over a road junction and after another $^1/_4$ mile see Christchurch campsite to the left. Go down to the corner of the campsite and turn right on a broad path that will lead you back to the Yat Rock (see Walk 49) car park.

REFRESHMENTS:
The refreshment hut in the car park is open during the summer months (March-October).
The Symonds Yat Motel (tel no: 0594 36191). Open for meals every day.
The Globe Inn, Berry Hill (tel no: 0594 32309). Bar meals available.

Maps: OS Sheets Landranger 162; Pathfinder ST 69/79.

An easy walk in all weathers, very suitable for children. The park is only open on Sundays.

Start: At 688923, see instructions below.

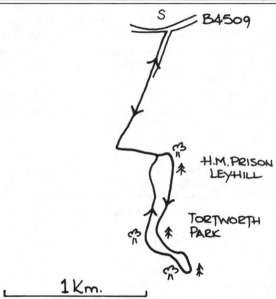

From Wotton-under-Edge take the B4058 to Charfield, then the B4509 towards Falfield and the M5. The lake is not actually signposted from the road, so be careful not to go too far. Drive down the lane to the left on the second bend before the motorway bridge, pass through two gates and past some farm buildings to the right. Cars may be parked by the wood sheds at the end of the track.

Go through the kissing gate by the wood sheds and follow the path through the woods to **Tortworth Lake** and the boathouse. The path follows the circumference of the lake so it is really your choice which way round to go. The lake is part of the Tortworth Estate and backs on to Leyhill Open Prison. Look out for the rhododendron bushes at the extreme end.

POINTS OF INTEREST:
Tortworth Lake – Open only on Sundays: October-March 10am-4.30pm; April-September 10am-7.30pm.

Walk 52 THE RIVER SEVERN NEAR SHEPPERDINE 3m (5km)

Maps: OS Sheets Landranger 162; Pathfinder ST 69/79.

A flat walk with fine views of the River Severn. This is <u>not</u> a circular route.

Start: At 613961, the Windbound Inn, Shepperdine.

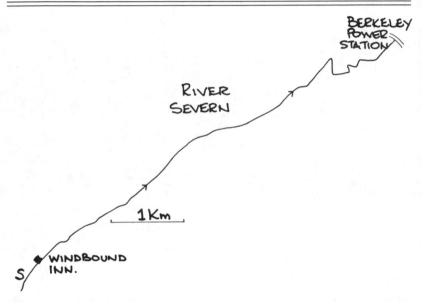

The walk begins along the obvious path passing in front of the pub in either direction. Left takes you along to Oldbury Nuclear Power Station for a shorter walk. You go right towards Berkeley. On a dull day this could be monotonous, but in the spring or height of summer it is extremely beautiful, with many varieties of wildfowl to be seen, all visitors to the nearby **Slimbridge Wildfowl Trust,** home of the late Sir Peter Scott.

A word of warning – do not attempt to go near or on to the mud flats at the edge of the river. The tides of the Severn are fast and very dangerous and there are quicksands in places.

The walk ends at **Berkeley Power Station,** and the path to be followed is marked by a blue arrow on a gate by the perimeter fence. This path can be overgrown in summer, but offers several interesting varieties of wildflower and you will probably see many rabbits. It emerges eventually after several twists and turns to the car park of the power station.

Note: If two cars are to be used to avoid a return walk the second should be left at some point along Ham Lane reached from the town of Berkeley.

POINTS OF INTEREST:
Slimbridge Wildfowl Trust – Needs little introduction. Open every day 9.30-4.30.
Berkeley Power Station – At present undergoing decommissioning, a process which could take up to 100 years. Visits can be arranged by phoning the station, or watch the local press for details of open days.

REFRESHMENTS:
The Windbound Inn, Shepperdine (tel no: 0454 414343). A selection of hot and cold meals and snacks. Children's play area.

Walk 53   **WOODMANCOTE AND DURSLEY**   3m (5km)

Maps: OS Sheets Landranger 162; Pathfinder ST 69/79.

An easy, varied and interesting walk with no steep gradients.

Start: At the New Inn, Woodmancote, an outlying area of Dursley.

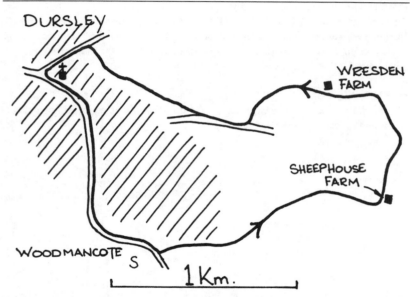

Follow the road up the hill, past Byron Close on your left and turn left down the bridleway marked 'Bowcote-Uley'. Follow the lane until it becomes a rough track. At a fork of three tracks, continue straight on to a gate and stile. Cross the stile and field and head towards the farm shortly visible ahead. Views here include the town of Dursley, Cam Peak and Uley Bury. Ignore the gate and stile to the left marked by a white arrow and head instead for a second gate and then a stile in the left-hand corner of the field, beneath a hedge. Follow the rough track down to the road past Sheephouse Farm. Cross the road and follow the drive up to Wresden Farm. Go through the gate just past the old cottage on the left and head through the paddocks behind the farm to a small gate beside the stream with barns on your right.

Steer a course straight across the fields, heading towards Mill Farm where a gate marked by a yellow arrow will bring you out into the farmyard. Notice on your left the waterfall below the farm. Continue up the drive between a cottage and large barn and turn right on to the main road. Follow the pavement along past Mawdsley's factory on the left and take the footpath which leads off to the right between the second cottage and the factory car park. This path runs alongside the stream and comes out on a small lane where you should turn right, past Kinver Grange and then continue to the factory yard. By keeping straight on you will reach the bottom of Long Street with the ancient **Priory** building on the right. Turn left up Long Street, where refreshments can be taken at the Old Bell, and at the Market Square, keep left past the church. Go straight on at the mini-roundabout and back into Woodmancote.

POINTS OF INTEREST:

The Priory – Dated above the main door as 1520, the home of the Webb family, Flemish weavers invited to England by Edward III and given a British name appropriate to their trade.

REFRESHMENTS:

The New Inn, Woodmancote (tel no: 0453 3001).
The Old Bell, Long Street (tel no: 0453 2821).

Maps: OS Sheets Landranger 162; Pathfinder ST 89/99.
An easy walk, through very pretty countryside. Dogs must be kept under control.
Start: Hunters Hall Inn on the A4135 Dursley to Tetbury road.

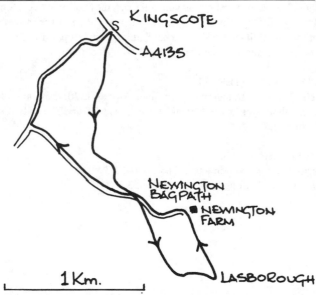

Standing with the front of the pub behind you, turn right and walk along the main road for approximately 100 yards. Pass through the small kissing gate in the wall just beyond the lane signposted to Bagpath, and skirt the field, keeping the wall on your right, to a large gate. Keeping straight ahead, with hawthorn bushes to the left, pass through a second gate and head downwards towards the stile taking you over a small stream. Turn left and at the copse of trees follow the track taking you through it. There are two gates on the track, the second opening into a large field with a view of the now disused **Newington Bagpath Church.** Head towards the church and follow the lane down to your left for 100 yards to a gate on the bank up to the right. Follow the line of fencing round the perimeter of the churchyard and, still in the same field, walk close to the wall to reach a gate. Notice here on your left the circular **Motte** and Newington Farm below.

The path now meanders gently down into the valley and the old manor house of **Lasborough** soon becomes visible. Head towards the house taking the path between the chestnut trees and poplars and emerge on the lane running past the house. Bear left over a cattle grid, up the lane past a cottage to the left, take the left track opposite a barn and shortly go right into a field. The path goes ahead of you slightly uphill and follows the contours of the hill until it drops down to meet a fence, and a gate between some hawthorns. Newington Farm is now visible again and you should steer a course for this, keeping to the edge of the field and passing around the perimeter of the walled garden to a gate leading on to a gravelled area and the lane. By turning left and continuing up the hill you are once again back at the old church. Follow the lane to a T-junction and turn right. This is a slightly meandering lane but in no time will bring you back to the Hunters Hall for that much needed drink!

POINTS OF INTEREST:

Newington Bagpath Church – Dedicated to St Bartholomew and now disused. The chancel was rebuilt in 1858. The tower is rendered with a hipped roof.

Motte – A deep, circular ditch 150 ft in diameter and 10-12 ft from the top of the mound to the bottom of the ditch.

Lasborough – The Manor was built around 1610 for Sir Thomas Estcourt.

REFRESHMENTS:

The Hunters Hall Inn (tel no: 0453 860393). Normal licensing hours, a good selection of hot and cold food, plus outdoor barbecues in the summer. There is a large garden equipped with children's adventure playground.

Walk 55 WOTTON HILL AND WOTTON-UNDER-EDGE 4m (6km)
Maps: OS Sheets Landranger 162; Pathfinder ST 69/79.
An interesting and varied walk around a Cotswold market town.
Start: In the centre of Wotton-under-Edge.

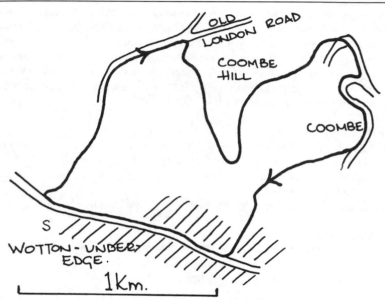

Walk along Market Street and turn left at the **Tolsey Clock** to reach the top of the High Street. Continue straight on up Bradley Street, bearing right at the top to bring you on to Gloucester Road. Turn left, then take the footpath with a handrail running sharply upwards at the base of the Old London Road. This path brings you on to Coombe Hill with its clump of walled trees and good views of the town and Severn Vale. Keep to the roadside edge of the hill with the woods to your right and cross a stile into a disused quarry area and on to the road. Turn left and walk straight on, taking the stile on the corner of the junction with a road down to the right. Follow this path through the woods, over a stile and around the edge of the hill to a third stile. Here, turn right down to the main road (B4058) and continue ahead down the opposite lane. Within 100 yards turn right and, shortly after, left, into the pretty hamlet of Coombe. Keep right to a T-junction. Turn left, then take the footpath ahead running alongside a stream through the meadows. This path crosses a lane at one point, but you should continue until it emerges at a wider junction. Bear left along Marchesi Walk. At the main road turn right and pass the ancient **Ram Inn**. A little further on, turn right at the War Memorial to visit **St Mary's Church**, or left up Church Street past **Hugh Perry's Almshouses,** to bring you back into the town.

POINTS OF INTEREST:
Tolsey Clock – A characteristic Jubilee clock, projecting over the High Street from the building which was at one time the town's lock-up.
Ram Inn – The oldest building in Wotton, reputed to have housed the builders of St Mary's Church.
St Mary's Church – Houses two magnificent brasses of Sir Thomas (Lord) Berkeley and his wife Margaret. These are said to date back to 1392 and so are possibly the earliest and most beautiful in the country.
Hugh Perry's Almshouses – Hugh Perry was born in Wotton and made Sheriff of London in 1632. The almshouses were built to house six poor men and six poor women of the town. An alleyway leads to a 17th-century chapel.

REFRESHMENTS:
The Falcon Inn, Church Street, Wotton-under-Edge (tel no: 0453 842138).
The Swan Inn, Market Street, Wotton-under-Edge (tel no: 0453 842329).
The Singing Teapot Café, Long Street, Wotton-under-Edge (tel no: 0453 844266).

Walk 56   HILL AND BEVINGTON   4m (6km)

Maps: OS Sheets Landranger 162; Pathfinder ST 69/79.

An easy walk, through fields and woodland. Views towards Bristol and the Severn Bridge.

Start: The small village of Hill, reached from Berkeley.

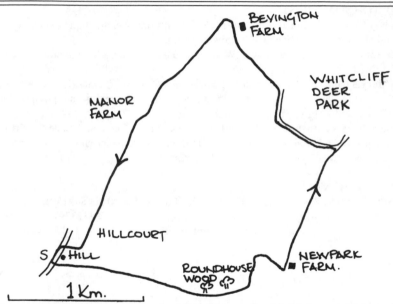

Go over the stile into the field to the right of the small red-brick house which stands alone to the right of the drive leading up to the church. Continue up the hill towards the copse of trees and then follow the line of fencing on your left to a gate. Turn left and follow the edge of the field and trees, downhill to a gate and small footbridge. Keeping the edge of the woods to your left, skirt the field around to a gate, crossing the next field in line with a large oak tree and then climbing up the bank to the edge of the woods where a small gate takes you into Roundhouse Wood. Follow a little-used path through the trees, predominantly oak and ash, and then take the small gate to your right into a field above Newpark Farm. Head down towards the gate on to the drive and turn left, continuing until the track meets the lane. Looking across to your right, notice the ridge of the Cotswold escarpment, with Nibley Knoll also visible.

At the end of the drive turn left up the grassy track by the house and continue upwards through the woods, turning right at the point where another track cuts across. Follow this very narrow path to a gate, emerging opposite a small deserted cottage and the perimeter wall of Whitcliff Deer Park. Pass in front of the cottage and continue down this field and diagonally down the next towards the track at the bottom of the ridge. Turn right on to the track and you will shortly be in the yard of Bevington Farm. After the last barn on your left turn up to your left through a small paddock and then diagonally down this field, heading towards Manor Farm.

There are two alternative return routes. Either go across the fields, keeping parallel with the road and crossing each field by means of gate or stile. You will eventually emerge into the beautiful parkland below Hill Court and a wooden gate on to the driveway to **Hill Church** which is well worth a visit. By continuing back down the drive you are once again back in the village. Otherwise, go along the lane from Bevington Farm.

Depending on the time of year, some of the fields may be inaccessible due to cultivation. In this case it is wiser to return to Hill by means of the second option.

POINTS OF INTEREST:
Hill Church – St Michael's, thought to date back to the 13th century.

Walk 57   SLIMBRIDGE TO CAMBRIDGE   4m (6km)

Maps: OS Sheets Landranger 162; Pathfinder SO 60/70.

A fairly easy walk with no steep inclines, but some muddy areas after rain.

Start: The church in the village of Slimbridge.

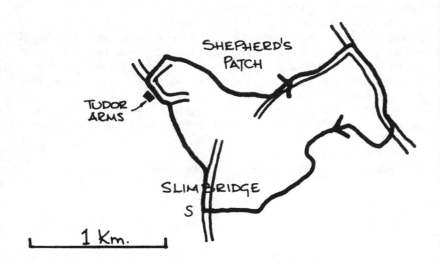

Leaving the church, walk back up the lane towards the A38, crossing the stile to your right beside Malthouse Farm. Cross the field to a gate and then keep the hedge to your left to a footbridge. Here, bear right, keeping to the right of some fencing, then left over a stile. Follow the fence as far as the corner and then cross the field and pass through a gate, bearing right and continuing across to a stile by a large tree. Keep straight on to a footbridge on to Lightenbrook Lane. Turn right and follow the lane along to a stile on your left. Go over and cross this field diagonally right, going over the small footbridge and steering the same course across the next field. Bear right through a gate on to the road. Turn left and continue along the lane to the Tudor Arms where you may wish to stop for refreshments.

Leaving the pub, continue along the lane opposite beside **Sharpness Canal**, past the youth hostel and over a stile towards a bungalow. Continue on to the corner of the field bearing right, then follow the ditch to the left. Cross two stiles and then turn left over a sleeper bridge before the road. Cross the stile over the track and bear right over the field to another stile by a tree. Continue over this next field to a stile emerging on to Longaston Lane. Turn left here and continue to the junction with Ryalls Lane where you should turn right. At the bend by Rolls Court turn right into the field and left along the path, keeping the ditch to your left. At the corner of the next field turn right, go through the gap in the hedge and on to a stile on the left. Go over and cross the field. Go through a gate and bear left to the corner of the churchyard. Follow the wall to the left and continue through the gate and on to the road, visiting the Church of St John *en route* .

PLACES OF INTEREST:
Sharpness Canal – Built in 1827; has a width of nearly 90 ft and a draught of 18 ft. It was once the largest ship canal in the world, able to take vessels weighing over 600 tons to the docks at Gloucester from the Bristol Channel.

REFRESHMENTS:
The Tudor Arms, Slimbridge (tel no: 045389 306).

Maps: OS Sheets Landranger 162; Pathfinder ST 69/79.

An easy and varied walk, with some beautiful views.

Start: The Church of St Giles in the village of Uley on the Dursley-Stroud road.

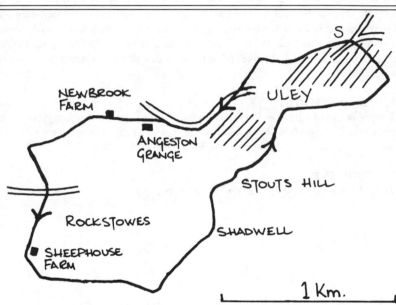

1 Km.

Take the footpath which runs behind Uley Church and eventually emerges on to a track. Take the path through the gate immediately ahead which skirts the fields behind a housing estate. Up above to your right is **Uley Bury.** Within $1/4$ mile a stile will bring you on to a rough lane leading to Whitecourt. Keep straight on past a variety of houses, small cottages and an old chapel on the left at a junction of the roads. This is Fop Street. By continuing on up the road you will find Angeston Grange and Nurseries on the left. Turn left down the track past the Nurseries to Newbrook Farm at the bottom and continue to follow this path until it emerges on to a small lane. Here, turn down to the left past Rockstowes House and on to the main road. Cross the road and go up the drive leading to Sheephouse Farm. At the top, opposite the house, cross the stile and keeping to the left pass through a gate marked by a yellow arrow. Continue diagonally across this small field through another gate and again bear left, following the yellow arrows, over a stile. Steer a course straight ahead aiming for the farm buildings shortly visible. The path now runs on to a gravel lane with cottages up to your right under the woods. Keep on along the lane passing through the hamlet of Elcombe, and from there down into Shadwell.

The lane does various twists and turns, passing by an **organic farm,** before emerging on to the bottom of the road leading up to Lampern Hill. Turn right and after approx 100 yards take the footpath to your left opposite the entrance to **Stouts Hill**. The path passes behind a cottage and a stile takes you into the fields with a stream on your left. Cross a second stile just to the right of the small footbridge and continue to follow this path keeping close to the stream's edge. The path passes through three fields by means of stile or gate, finally bringing you to another stone footbridge which you should cross. Continue straight ahead, aiming for the houses at the top of the field by the large oak tree and passing over another small brook. A stile at this point and a narrow path will bring you on to a gravelled area between two cottages on the village green. By turning left you will find the Old Crown on your left and the church to your right.

POINTS OF INTEREST:

Uley – The village is the home of the Prema Arts Centre, up the lane opposite the Post Office. The Centre has a varied timetable of events throughout the year including performance, exhibitions and childrens workshops (tel no: 0453 860703/860800).

Uley Bury – Iron Age hill fort with clearly defined ramparts.

Organic farm – Sells a variety of organically-grown produce, plants and tubs. Open most days.

Stouts Hill – Built around 1740 and for many years the private home of the Lloyd-Baker family. It became a private school and one famous pupil was Mark Phillips. More latterly it has become a holiday ownership resort with the building divided into apartments.

REFRESHMENTS:

The Old Crown Inn, Uley (tel no: 0453 860502).

Walk 59   SELSLEY AND WOODCHESTER   4m (6.5km)

Maps: OS Sheets Landranger 162; Pathfinder SO 80/90.

An easy walk but not level and with wet muddy patches.

Start: At 829027, near the portaloo on Selsley Common.

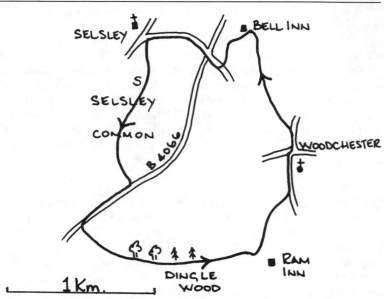

From the portaloo (only open Easter to October) walk beside the B4066 towards Dursley and just before the cattle grid turn left on to a footpath signposted 'Woodchester'. Descend to Dingle Wood and hold the left boundary through a field, a new copse and then take the left fork of the cart-track to a road. (This road leads down to the Ram Inn and **South Woodchester,** and opposite the inn is a lane leading to St Mary the Virgin Church.)

The walk continues via the footpath just below 'Wingletang' on the left, which descends a field, crosses Laggar Lane into parkland and continues down over a stream before climbing to St Mary the Virgin church. Go along Church Road; past 'Home Ground' and Berrimore Road is the Royal Oak Inn. Turn right out of Church Road, then immediately left. A short distance on your left past 'Roman Way' is the graveyard site of the famous **Woodchester Pavement.** It is beneath the sunken area and was discovered by grave diggers. Just before the graveyard, turn left into a walled footpath. Keep to the right-hand boundary through the field, and go up through the copse, over two fields to a cart-track. The Bell Inn is at the end of this cart-track. Turn left up the field and left into a private drive. Veer into the right-hand field to reach Water Lane. Turn right, uphill, and continue over crossroads to **Selsley Church**. Opposite the Monument is a footpath which climbs gradually (below old quarries) to the top of Selsley Common. Veer left at the top towards the farm and the portaloo.

POINTS OF INTEREST:
South Woodchester – A very interesting cluster of old residences around the shop/ Post Office.
The Woodchester Pavement – A 4th-century Romano- British mosaic, the largest and most complex one in Europe, north of the Alps, and last opened to the public in 1973. Since then John and Bob Woodward of Wotton-under-Edge have built an excellent replica entitled the 'Wotton Mosaic' which has been on display in Wotton, Bath and Stroud. It is currently homeless and awaiting decisions on a permanent site in the Stroud area.
Selsley Church – Believed to be based on a church in the old Tyrolean village of Marling, it was the idea of Sir Samuel Stephens Marling who resided at Stanley Park. It was built in 1862.

REFRESHMENTS:
The Bell Inn (tel no: 04536 4910).
The Ram Inn (tel no: 045387 3329).
The Royal Oak (tel no: 045387 2735).

Walk 60 ASTON DOWN TO FRAMPTON MANSELL 4m (6.5km)
Maps: OS Sheets Landranger 163; Pathfinder SO 80/90.
Through woods and beside the Thames and Severn Canal.
Start: At 912019, the lay-by by Aston Down airfield, at the top of
Cowcombe Hill on the A419.

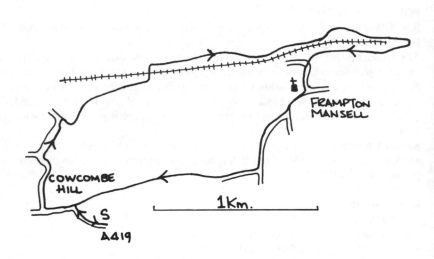

Proceed along the A419 towards Chalford and on the first bend take the minor road, marked 'No vehicle over 7'6"', left. In 150 yards turn right, past Herb Farm on your left, and proceed down to main road. Cross over this road (it is safer to walk on the right-hand side) and proceed downhill round the bend for about 100 yards. Be very careful on this stretch as there is a lot of traffic. Opposite Cowcombe House, turn right down a steep lane and proceed to where it bends left. On your right are two gates. Take the first, marked 'Westley Walk'. (This is not a recognised public Right of Way but the walker is welcome to use it and we would advise careful use of this privilege.) Proceed downhill and at the end of the fence on the right, turn half-right downhill to the bottom of the valley. Still following waymarks, go left, climbing steadily to arrive at a facing wood. Enter Westley Wood and follow the well-worn footpath. After about ¹/₂ mile you will climb a slope for about 100 yards. At this point a fence from the left comes up to the path: cross the stile left and descend a steep slope to cross the Gloucester-Swindon railway line. Follow the path round to the right and descend to the road – the end of the Westley Walk.

Turn right and in 75 yards go left on a path over a footbridge to cross the old **Thames and Severn Canal**. Turn right on to the old towpath. This path is in good order and will be followed for about 1 mile. At about the $^1/_2$ mile mark you will pass through a gate. Cross the canal bridge and proceed ahead on the other side of the canal. Continue ahead and enter a wooded area where you will come to a red-brick canal bridge with the sign 'WD 1784' on it. At this point, leave the canal and turn right. At the first fork, after a few yards, turn right. This is a well-used bridle path and could be muddy in winter. After $^1/_4$ mile you will pass through an iron gate into a field. Still follow the track to reach railway gates. Pass through these gates (beware of trains) and on to a hard track. In 100 yards go on to a metalled road, and turn left up into Frampton Mansell.

The Crown Inn is to the left. Pass it, turn right and take the main Stroud road through the village (keep left by the phone box). After about $^1/_4$ mile, having passed the last houses of the village on your left (The Hollies/Four Ways), look for a bridle path right. Go through and, following the track, make for the farm buildings ahead. You should have a wall left all the way across here. Pass the farm buildings on your left and descend the last field to the road. Pass through a gate and turn left to go back to the starting point.

POINTS OF INTEREST:
Thames and Severn Canal – Opened in 1789 the canal fell into disuse in 1933. A canal trust is slowly bringing this back to life, and it is full of interesting wildlife.

REFRESHMENTS:
The Crown Inn, Frampton Mansell (tel no: 028576 218).

Walk 61 THE STROUDWATER VALLEY, ROUTE 1 4m (6.5km)

Maps: OS Sheets Landranger 162; Pathfinder SO 80/90.

Climbing the valley's flank and returning along the Thames and Severn Canal.

Start: At 867025, a lay-by on the A419 near Brimscombe Football Ground.

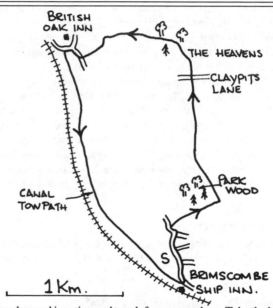

Walk towards the nearby road junction and turn left up a steep lane. Take the left branch at a fork, and a little further on bear left at a T-junction. About 150 yards from the junction pass Shilliams Cottage and immediately cross a stile on the right and walk up the path beyond. When confronted by a sign 'Private', move a few yards right and resume the climb up the field's edge. Go through a gap at the end of a fence and bear slightly right so that you draw gradually away from the left-hand field boundary. Aim for a house and as you near the top of the field a stile will be seen. Go over this and turn right on a narrow path. In about 30 yards it merges with a wider track but keep on to the next junction where you turn sharply left. Walk 60 yards up a rise to a gate with a stile alongside. Climb over this and emerge into an open space. 120 yards ahead is the corner of a wood. A stile here gives access to a path along the edge of Park Wood. There is another stile about half-way and at the other end you emerge into a field.

Go straight across the field to a 'V' stile in the wall opposite. Maintain the line to a stile on to Claypits Lane. Across the lane negotiate a stone stile and walk diagonally over a field towards the houses of 'The Heavens'. Crossing the stile in the corner, move slightly left and walk down a driveway that is first tarmac surfaced then concrete, finally becoming a stony track. Entering a wood, the track divides, rejoining a little further on. The track steepens and after a stile, you will descend to a kissing gate and emerge into an open space. Proceed in the same line, keeping right of a group of trees. Walk on to the bottom corner and after crossing a footbridge turn left through a gap in the bushes. After 40 yards cross another footbridge and, bearing right, walk diagonally across and up, gradually drawing away from the stream to the right. The track is not too obvious, but after about 150 yards you should see a narrow extension to the field ahead. Walk down this to a stile, and on beyond to a T-junction where you should go right down Gunhouse Lane. After 70 yards bear right along the A419 to a crossroads. Taking care, cross the road and walk down the left turn to where the road crosses a canal (see Walk 60). Go down some steps on the left and walk along the towpath. As the path nears Brimscombe the canal vanishes where it has been built over, and just before the road is reached by the Ship Inn, the towpath has itself become a road. Turn left, and at the junction with the A419 go left again. Walk along the main road a short distance and return to the starting point.

REFRESHMENTS:
The Ship Inn, Brimscombe (tel no: 0453 884388). Bar meals.
The British Oak Inn, Bowbridge, Stroud (tel no: 0453 766802). Snacks.

Walk 62   ALDERLEY AND TRESHAM   4¹/₂m (7km)

Maps: OS Sheets Landranger 162; Pathfinder ST 69/79.

An easy walk with undulating gradients, mainly through fields.
Start: At 769910, in the lane going east, just north of Alderley village.

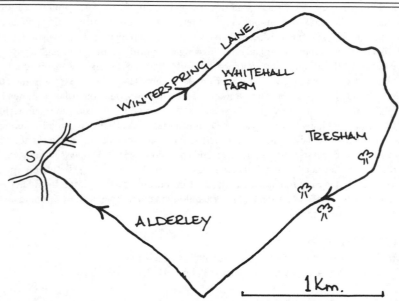

Walk eastwards from your car to a small crossroads. Turn left. Take the next right down a farm lane signposted to Alderley and Oldown Farms. This is Winterspring Lane which leads through the middle of the farmyard, so beware of mud and some pungent aromas! Carry on past Whitehall Farm on the left, where the track ends. Go over a stile and into a field. Keep straight ahead to a gate into a second field and walk diagonally right to a stile. Go over on to a gravel track. The views here include the Ozleworth Valley and **Ozleworth Tower.** Continue up the track until you reach a gate and a fork in the ways. Keep straight on to a gate ahead of you on a right-hand bend. Cross the field to a stile and a small path alongside a converted barn. This emerges in the yard of a house, beyond which is a lane running through the village of Tresham.

Take the path running down into the valley immediately opposite, keeping the

132

fence to your right and continue walking until you reach a gate and track. About 100 yards further on, fork right by a gate and keep along this path which follows the contours of the hill and skirts various small fields. There are four gates to pass through in total: the last one will bring you out into a yard with a barn on the left and sheds up to the right. The path now passes in front of a large country house and emerges back on the main B4060. Turn right and then left to arrive back at your car, or follow the main road round to visit the church before returning to the start. Just north of the start is the **Alderly Trout Farm**.

Note: Please keep dogs under control at all times, as there is plenty of livestock on this walk!

POINTS OF INTEREST:

Alderley Trout Farm – Farm shop, open Monday-Saturday, 10am-5.30 pm for fresh or smoked trout (tel no: 0453 842540).

Ozleworth Tower – Post office tower, a smaller edition of the London tower, built about 1965.

Walk 63 THE STROUDWATER VALLEY, ROUTE 2 4¹/₂m (7km)
Maps: OS Sheets Landranger 162; Pathfinder SO 80/90.
By the Thames and Severn Canal, then through fields.
Start: At 867025, a lay-by on the A419 near Brimscombe Football
Ground.

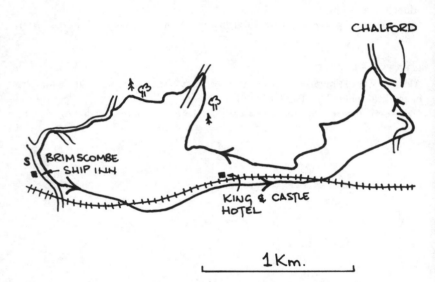

Cross the road and walk left towards a road junction. Bear right along the road towards
Minchinhampton and after passing the Ship Inn start to go uphill. After a few yards bear
left off the road to the side of Bensons factory. Soon you can move left on to a roadway
along the bank of the River Frome. Presently the road narrows to a track then moves
away from the river and the disused canal (see Walk 60) appears on the left. Stay on
the towpath with the canal to the left and, at times, the River Frome to the right. Shortly
after passing under the railway for the second time some steps lead up to a road. Walk
along this for 50 yards and rejoin the towpath to the left. This soon goes past a
roundhouse then rises to a crossroads by Chalford Church.

Go across the A419 and up the road called Old Neighbourhood with the church
to your left. Where the road bends left, go straight ahead up a narrow lane which rejoins

134

the road higher up. Walk up the road a further 150 yards to where a finger post points to two footpaths to the left. Take the one making the sharper turn and cross a stile by a gate. Cross the field to a kissing gate near the top corner of the field and then go across the next field to a stile near its upper corner. Beyond a stile 100 yards away, across a further field, you will encounter a surfaced drive. Bear right up it to a stile by a gate. The Right of Way now goes through the grounds of the nearby house, keeping well to the left and finally up the drive to an exit on to a road (Skaites Hill). Turn left down the hill to where the lane bends left, then going right, through an entrance marked 'Firwood', immediately bear left down a track. Where this bends left and forks, take the left-hand, narrower path down to a stile, beyond which turn very sharply right to pass just above 'Edge Hill'. Keeping near the right-hand boundary go over a stile and, a little further on, over another stile. Cross another stile just beyond a small stream then go through a 'V' stile in the right-hand fence. The path beyond hugs the fence for a few yards until open ground is reached, then begins to climb obliquely across the bank. Go up to a metal gate and beyond go steeply up at about 45 degrees to the fence to where a well-defined path comes down from right to left. Crossing this, look for a continuation path across the hillside to the corner where you will find a stile. Crossing this, descend steeply for a few feet to a lane and turning left follow the lane as it bends first right then left. Below this you will see a direction post pointing to a footpath to Bussage.

Turn right up a drive for a few yards and take the footpath to the left. Follow this through a wood and at a junction fork right up to a stile. After 30 yards another stile leads to a drive. Go left down to the road to Eastcombe and turn sharp left along it until you see a driveway to the right marked 'The Cottage – Lawrenceland'. Walk up this to a cattle grid then over a stile to the right and up the field to a gate at the top. A few yards higher, go over a stile and turn left along a track for 100 yards. Where this kinks left, go right and almost straight up the bank. There is a spinney at the top and yellow arrows point a way through to a stile at the upper edge. Go over the following field to a gate to the right of the furthest house, then bear left down a narrow footpath to a lane. Go left for 20 yards then right down a footpath. At the end turn left down a lane, bear right at a junction then turn left and keep going down to the A419. Go right to the car park.

POINTS OF INTEREST:
Roundhouse – One of five watchmen's dwellings along the length of the canal.

REFRESHMENTS:
The Ship Inn, Brimscombe (tel no: 0453 884388). Bar meals.
The King and Castle Hotel, Brimscombe (tel no: 0453 883619). Bar meals.

Maps: OS Landranger Sheets 162 & 163; Pathfinder Sheet SO 80/90.

A wooded valley and fields with fine views.

Start: Near the Post Office and the Lamb Inn, Eastcombe.

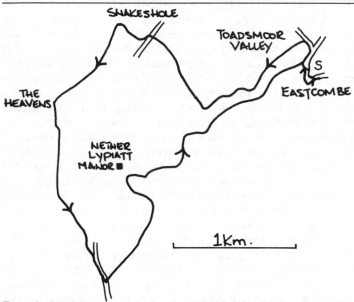

From the Lamb Inn turn right down a lane before the Baptist church, then turn sharp right by Chancewell Cottage. Continue downhill by a zig-zag route until you cross the stream by a bridge. Descend left by the stream and follow it, and then Toadsmoor Lake, to the end. Turn right up a cart-track. Continue along a footpath, cross a stream, climb a stile and turn left up the field to a stile in the middle of the top boundary. Continue along a walled track to Middle Lypiatt and on to a road. Turn left for 50 yards and then right through Woodland Cottage gates and into a field. Before the stile, turn left along the right boundary and left through a field gate on to the drive and footpath above the garage of Woodland Cottage. Climb the stile and keep to the left boundary of the next two fields. Cross the lane into a field and head half-right for a stile in the opposite boundary. Cross the next field diagonally to a stile in the bottom corner, approaching

'The Heavens'. At the junction, turn left over a stile and ascend the field diagonally to a stone slab stile and the lane.

Take the footpath opposite across the field due south to the squeezer stile and straight on across the next field to a stile at the top of a wood. Keep to the left boundary in the wood but beyond take the path half-right below a quarry and continue south by a cart-track. At Quarhouse take the right fork and descend to a finger post and footpath on the left between houses. Then descend the lane for 20 yards and turn left along another footpath. Cross tracks and a stile into the field, keeping to the left through the first field and cross the middle of the next two fields. At a double stile take the upper path, keeping above the right boundary to a stile and footpath above a cottage. Descend some small steps and proceed along the drive. At the cross-lanes continue with the wall on your left. About 25 yards before the end of the wall an **obelisk** may be seen 50 yards above the track among the trees. Descend along the muddy main track to the corner of a wood and take the left fork which leads you down a footpath to cottages.

Continue over the stream to a T-junction and ascend the footpath opposite. Turn left on to a track just before the road and after $^3/_4$ mile look for 5 steps and a stile on the right. Ascend by the right boundary of the field to the stile which you passed during the descent from the Lamb Inn. Follow the road back up to the village green.

POINTS OF INTEREST:
The Obelisk – This has a verse on it commemorating Wag, a horse which lived for 42 years.

REFRESHMENTS:
The Lamb Inn, Eastcombe (tel no: 0452 770261).

Walk 65   BROOKEND TO SHARPNESS   5m (8km)

Maps: OS Sheets Landranger 162; Outdoor Leisure 14.

A pleasant walk with good views of the River Severn.

Start: Lammastide Inn, in the hamlet of Brookend, near Berkeley.

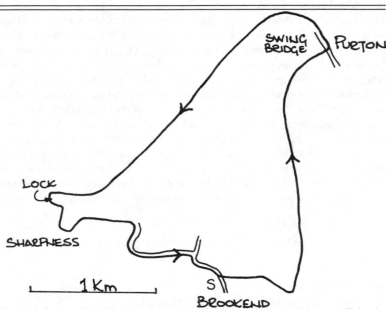

Walk down the lane past the pub to the end of the row of terraced houses. Take the second track right after the last house and within 100 yards pass through the right-hand gate of two, into a field. Keep close to the left side of the field to a gate marked by a yellow arrow. The path crosses a field to a gate (in summer, corn may impede your passage so skirt the edge of the field to the left) and from there the course to be followed is basically straight ahead through five more gates, each clearly marked by a yellow arrow. The last gate will bring you into a wide open field overlooking the village of Purton and the wide expanse of river. To your right is the Sharpness Canal (see Walk 57). Cross the field diagonally down towards the houses (again there is a likelihood of crops in summer, so be prepared to skirt!) and take the gate to the left of a small bungalow. The path emerges on to the road between the church and a red-brick house. Turn left to the road junction, then right over the swing bridge to the Berkeley Hunt Inn.

Leaving the pub, follow the towpath over the lane, towards the river and continue to follow this easy path into Sharpness Marina, a distance of approx $1^1/_2$ miles. Notice *en route* the abandoned hulks of concrete and wooden river barges left on the river banks to prevent erosion by the tides. Also note the ruins of the **Severn Railway Bridge.** At the marina take the small swing bridge at its extreme end. Go up some steps and on to the lane running past the Docker's Clubhouse. At the bottom bear left up a new road to go over a large swing bridge and on up to a sharp right-hand bend. Turn left at the next junction, then right at a T-junction to arrive back in Brookend.

POINTS OF INTEREST:
Severn Railway Bridge – The bridge was opened in 1897. It was 22 spans wide until November 1959 when two oil tankers heading for Sharpness collided and demolished the two central spans. Both crews were killed in the ensuing fire.

REFRESHMENTS:
The Lammastide Inn, Brookend (tel no: 0453 811337).
The Berkeley Hunt, Purton (tel no: 0453 810239).

Walk 66   **WATERLEY BOTTOM**   5m (8km)

Maps: OS Sheets Landranger 162; Pathfinder ST 69/79.

A fairly strenuous walk with one area of steep gradient.

Start: At 758944, near 'The House that Jack built' (a local name) on the Old London Road out of Wotton-under-Edge.

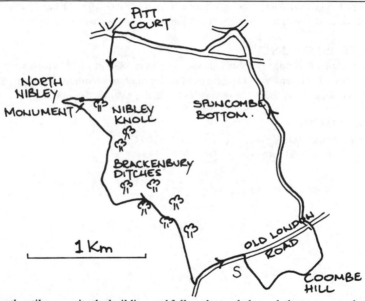

Cross the stile opposite the building and follow the track through the trees on to the hill, bearing round to the left over a stile to follow the ridge of the hill. Notice down to your right the **strip lynchets** and pleasant views of the Coombe Valley. At the third stile turn left up a stony path to bring you back on to the Old London Road. Take the path opposite signed to Spuncombe Bottom and after 100 yards veer right and then left at the next fork continuing on down to emerge on the lane known as 'The Throat'. Turn right and follow this twisting, sometimes muddy lane to a crossroads, continuing straight ahead following signs to the New Inn. You will shortly find this pub tucked under the lee of the hill with pleasant views across the valley.

    Leaving the pub, walk back down the lane to the small grass triangle and here bear right, then almost immediately left, passing a roadside stream and continuing up the hill to a T-junction. Turn right and follow the lane for about $3/4$ mile to an island with a telephone kiosk and opposite two gates. Cross the stile to the right of the second gate, following the path to a field which you should cross diagonally up and to the left to a gate and stile. Continue around the edge of the woods for approximately 100 yards, taking the path to your right up into the woods. At the point where a wider path cuts across this one, continue straight up to a gate which emerges on the top of Nibley Knoll. Skirt the disued quarry to the right and head for **Tyndale's Monument**. Views from here include the Malverns and the Black Mountains of Wales.

Leaving the monument, follow the edge of the escarpment round to a copse of beech trees and once through the gate, turn right. Take the last track to the left and continue on to a large clearing which marks the site of **Brackenbury Ditches.** Keep straight on, bearing right at the next fork along the edge of the hill, and right again on to a path which eventually brings you back to the Old London Road. Turn right to go back to the starting point.

POINTS OF INTEREST:

Strip lynchets – Ancient form of terracing a hillside to gain maximum use from the land.

Tyndale's Monument – Monument to the translator of the Bible from German into English. Keys for access to the monument may be obtained from the village shop on leaving a small deposit.

Brackenbury Ditches – Iron Age hill fort which encloses approximately 8 acres.

REFRESHMENTS:

The New Inn, Waterley Bottom (tel no: 0453 3659). The winner of many awards for its gardens. Serves an excellent menu and welcomes children (playground provided).

Walk 67   EAST DEAN   5m (8km)

Maps: OS Sheets Landranger 162; Outdoor Leisure 14.

A walk through woodlands, beginning and ending by the delightful Soudley Ponds.

Start: At 661118, a car park on Soudley to Littledean road.

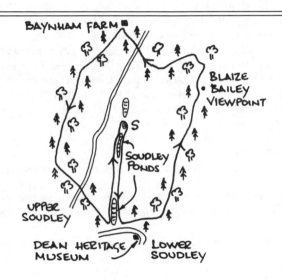

Leave the car park and coming back down the track, go right then left to gain a broad forestry road that goes past the eastern shores of the three lower ponds. Just short of the gate to the road go left (*not* hard left up the steps), and climb gradually up through woodland. This part of the walk is waymarked by posts, each with a fluorescent green band round the top. The path levels out and turns north. At one point it runs parallel to a broad forestry road and then turns to join it. Walk along the forestry road for perhaps 100 yards then go right (note the waymarking) on a path that again runs parallel to the main road. Turn right soon and you will shortly emerge at the **Blaize Bailey** viewpoint. This is as far as the green banded posts will take you.

    With your back to the view, go slightly right and bear right again along the main forestry road. As this road starts to bend left, go straight ahead, on a lesser track towards a house, but turn left just before the building. Now descend, keeping generally near the edge of the woodland and crossing two stiles. At one point you will cross the bottom of a shallow valley then climb briefly before descending again to the road.

Cross the road and climb the stile on the other side. Now go up the slope following a barely discernible path. Cross a horizontal track and head for the top right-hand corner of the field. A stile opposite a hay barn will give you access to a track that ascends to the left. This climbs steadily to a Y-junction where you should go slightly left of straight ahead on a broad track that now gradually descends. Follow this for rather more then $^1/_2$ mile to a four-way junction marked by three tall beeches. Turn left down the slope, crossing a forestry road. Bear right where it merges with another track and soon you will cross the Soudley/Littledean lane. Keep on in line and you will shortly come down by the foot of the Lower Soudley pond. Return to the car park by taking the path up the western side of the lower three ponds.

POINTS OF INTEREST:
Blaize Bailey – A viewpoint prepared by the Forestry Commission. It looks towards the Cotswolds but the main feature is the great horseshoe bend of the River Severn.

REFRESHMENTS:
The White Horse Inn, Soudley (tel no: 0594 22380). Bar meals available.
The Dean Heritage Museum, a little way to the east of the Soudley Café (tel no: 0594 22170). At the museum there are displays of forest life with reconstructed buildings, craft workshops, a millpond, a waterwheel and woodcraft exhibits. Open daily throughout the year.

Walk 68   CAM PEAK TO ULEY BURY   5$\frac{1}{2}$m (9km)

Maps: OS Sheets Landranger 162; Pathfinder ST69/79.

A relatively strenuous walk with some steep ascents and descents. Dogs must be kept under control.

Start: At 766991, the foot of Cam Peak to the east of Cam village.

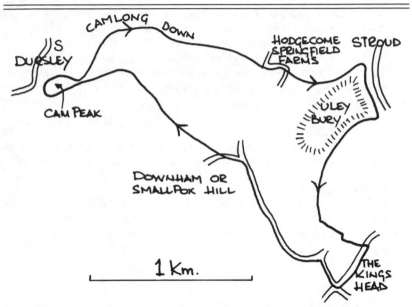

The **Cam Peak** itself is the obvious first goal. It offers magnificent views of the Berkeley Vale and River Severn. From the top, the spiny ridge of **Cam Long Down** can be seen stretching away to the north, while to the north-east is the tree-topped mound of **Downham Hill,** known locally as Smallpox Hill. Take the path off the Peak towards the Down and upwards between the bracken on to the ridge. Follow the ridge to its furthermost end where the path dips steeply down to a small sheepgate and a large terraced field. The route is clear to see from here, down through the field to a small stile leading on to a narrow lane. At the top of this lane, bear left up a gravel track towards Hodgecombe and Springfield Farms. The path here narrows and winds upwards through the woods at the base of Uley Bury (see Walk 58). At the top is a gate and the main Dursley to Stroud road (B4066). Go through the gate, turn right along a short

144

track, on to a small car park, then straight on. You are now on the ramparts of Uley Bury itself and can walk around the complete fort if desired. For the purposes of this walk follow the ramparts round to the second corner, then take the narrow path down off the Bury shortly after the spot where the trees clear and Uley village becomes visible down to the left.

This path will bring you down to a large field, and a stile leading on to a metalled path. At the bottom go over another stile into 'Whitecourt'. Turn left, pass the **Uley Brewery** and then turn right just before the main road. Bear left through a small council estate and find the King's Head pub on your left.

Leaving the pub, turn left and then right up the fairly steep Fop Street. Follow the lane round to the left, past the Angeston Nurseries, until within 1 mile you reach Hydegate Kennels on a small crossroads. Turn left here and then directly right down a signed footpath, over the footbridge at the bottom, and then straight on until you again reach the lower slopes of Cam Peak and your original starting point.

POINTS OF INTEREST:

Cam Peak and Cam Long Down – A service of witness is held on top of the Peak every Good Friday. Cam Long Down was once part of the main Cotswold escarpment, but erosion has separated it from the neighbouring uplands.

Downham Hill – This was once the site of an isolation hospital for smallpox victims in the 18th century. It has been said that the hill itself is a burial ground with the trees planted on top as a memorial.

The Uley Brewery – Well known for its selection of ales, and supplier to many local hostelries.

REFRESHMENTS:

The King's Head, Uley (tel no: 0453 860282). Provides a good lunch-time menu.

Walk 69 THE TIP OF THE HORSESHOE 6m (9.5km)

Maps: OS Sheets Landranger 162; Pathfinder SO 61/71 & 60/70.

A walk round part of the 'inside' of the famous Horseshoe Bend of the River Severn

Start: At 708109, near the crossroads in Arlingham village.

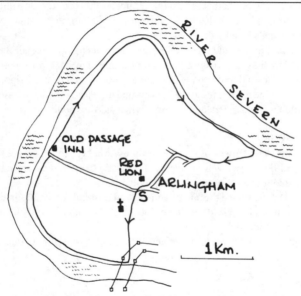

Go down the road opposite the Red Lion, passing the church to the right. In a little under $^1/_2$ mile, where the road bends right, go straight ahead through a gate and keep on the same line until you reach the flood-retaining embankment just to the left of a tall pylon. Turn right and walk along the crest of the embankment. You are now on the River Severn Path and you will encounter several fences, which are all crossed by stiles. After just over 1 mile of river bank the end of a road is reached near the Old Passage. There are views across river to the village of Newnham.

Proceed along the embankment and you will soon see the spire of Westbury Church ahead. Rounding a bend you walk opposite the **Garden Cliff** of grey and pink stone. Almost 3 miles from the Old Passage look for a stile with a footpath sign pointing right. When you have crossed the stile there should be just one fence before the near

146

riverside pylon. Follow the track that bends round to the right. In little more than 100 yards turn right through a gate and cross a field to a footbridge. Keeping to the right-hand hedge cross three fields with stiles between them. After the third stile bear slightly right down a lane and turn left after 100 yards into another lane. Follow this until you meet the main road and go right for a few yards, back to your starting point.

POINTS OF INTEREST:
The electricity pylons where the cables cross the river to the south of Arlingham are 292ft high.
Garden Cliff – It is said that stone from here was used to build Odda's Chapel at Deerhurst, near Tewkesbury.

REFRESHMENTS:
The Red Lion Inn, Arlingham (tel no: 0452 740269). Bar meals daily.
The Old Passage Inn, Arlingham (tel no: 0452 740547). Bar meals and restaurant.

Walk 70 **NEWARK PARK AND OZLEWORTH BOTTOM** $6\frac{1}{2}$m (10km)
Maps: OS Sheets Landranger 162; Pathfinder ST 69/79.
A varied walk with interesting features and fine views. Wellingtons might be advisable!
Start: At 764922, on the Alderley road from Wotton-under-Edge, opposite a turning to Nind.

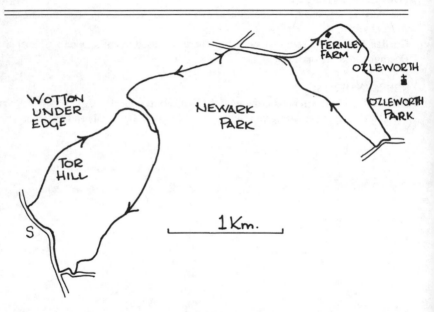

Take the track through the woods to the left marked for Tor Hill. At the top two gates bring you into a field which should be crossed diagonally to a gate in the far corner. Skirt the edge of the next field to another gate marked by a blue arrow and continue straight ahead, following the line of fencing to the point where it joins a wall. There is a raised water tank to the left and shortly after a gate you come on to a track. Go down this track as far as the lane, then bear right and continue to a junction where you should again turn right. The lane takes you past the gates to **Newark Park**. Notice also Ozleworth Tower (see Walk 62), over to the left.

Follow the lane round through a gate and past Fernley Farm down in the valley. A second gate will bring you out on to a lane by a telephone kiosk. Bear right and continue walking to the large gates of Ozleworth Park. Pass through the gates down the drive towards the house. The path to be followed is just short of the house following the line of fencing down into the woods on the right. At this stage you can visit **Ozleworth Church** by walking round in front of the house, between the old barns.

To continue the walk, carry on down through the woods, forking right at the bottom to a Gothic-style gatehouse. Go through the gate and turn right on to the lane. Within 100 yards turn left up into the woods and pass through a gate into a field. It is important here to keep close to the edge of the wall as it is covered by undergrowth in parts and the stile into the next field may be missed. Again keep close to the wall right up to the copse and finally over one more stile into a triangular-shaped field. Aim for the house at the top of the field, but be aware of any crops growing here. A stile next to the house leads on to the lane by the gates of Newark Park. Retrace your steps back along the lane, bearing left at the junction, and then left again back down the track to Tor Hill. At the fork with the gate, bear left and follow the path around to a junction of paths. Follow the arrows right, down a small path through the woods until it reaches a wider track. Turn left to the lane and then right into Wortley. At the T-junction go right and follow the road back for approximately $^1/_2$ mile to your car.

POINTS OF INTEREST:
Newark Park – Reputed to have been built with the stones from Kingswood Abbey which was demolished around 1540. Note the large Gothic porch. A National Trust property. House and gardens open April, May, August and September, Wednesdays and Thursdays 2pm-5pm.
Ozleworth Church – St Nicholas' church has a rare hexagonal tower dating from around 1131.

REFRESHMENTS:
The Fleece, Hillesley (tel no: 0453 843189).
The Portcullis, Hillesley (tel no: 0453 842313).

Walk 71   BERKELEY TO HAM   6½m (10km)

Maps: OS Sheets Landranger 162; Pathfinder ST 69/79.

A long attractive walk with some interesting views.

Start: The small town of Berkeley.

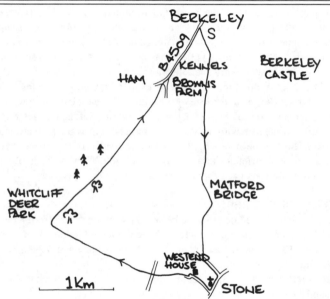

Walk out of the town on the B4509 towards Ham and Stone. Pass by the entrance to the **Jenner Museum**, then take the path signposted to Woodford, opposite a playing field. Cross the field diagonally right towards the trees and keep to the path which follows the edge of the Little Avon River. Looking back, there is a magnificent view of **Berkeley Castle**: the sound of barking dogs comes from the Berkeley Hunt Kennels. Keep the river to your right and follow the yellow arrows past Brownsmill Farm and over several stiles, eventually reaching Matford Bridge which is large and gated. Cross this. Keep the river close to your left and cross the stile in the corner of the field. Turn right and follow the field round to a gate. From here, steer a course straight ahead towards the spire of Stone Church. A large stile will bring you out on to the road where you should turn left.

At the main A38 turn right and right again by the church and village green.

Continue straight down the lane marked as 'No Through Road' to Westend House, and turn left along the bridleway. Follow this down to a lane. Cross the lane and take the opposite path down as far as a footbridge into a field. Cross this field diagonally left to a stile and walk straight on over fields via two more stiles to a second lane. Here, turn right then almost immediately left over a stile and up along the edge of a field to yet another stile marked by a yellow arrow. Follow the arrow sharply right and up the bank to a small path hidden in undergrowth skirting a red-brick wall (this is the perimeter wall of **Whitcliff Deer Park**). Enter the park over a large stile by a derelict cottage. The path now takes you the full length of this ridge, affording marvellous views of the River Severn and Berkeley Power Station. Notice also the small castellated Park Lodge. At the extreme end the path drops to a kissing gate stile by the old gatehouse and emerges on the Berkeley-Stone road once more. Continue ahead into Ham and stop for refreshments at the Salutation, or carry on back into Berkeley for a well-earned rest.

POINTS OF INTEREST:

Jenner Museum – Edward Jenner (the discoverer of the smallpox vaccine) was born in the Old Vicarage here in 1749. The hut in which he carried out his vaccinations is by the rectory wall bordering the churchyard. Opening times are 12.30-5.30, Tuesday-Saturday, 1.00-5.30, Sundays. Closed on Mondays (except Bank Holidays).

Berkeley Castle – Scene of Edward II's murder. Open from 1 April or Good Friday to 30 September except Mondays. April-September, 2pm-5pm; May-August, Tuesday-Saturday, 11am-5pm, Sundays, 2pm-5pm. Bank Holiday Mondays, 11am-5pm (October-Sundays only).

Whitcliff Deer Park – The park was first enclosed by Lord Maurice of Berkeley in 1243 and covers 325 acres. *Note* : It is imperative to keep to the footpath through the park at all times in order not to disturb the deer. Dogs must be kept under *strict* control.

REFRESHMENTS:

The Salutation, Ham (tel no: 0453 810284).
Numerous in Berkeley.

Walk 72   SOUTH-EAST DEAN FOREST   6¹/₂ m (10km)

Maps: OS Sheets Landranger 162; Outdoor Leisure 14.

An undulating walk almost entirely through mixed forest.

Start: At 637092, the car park at Mallards Pike.

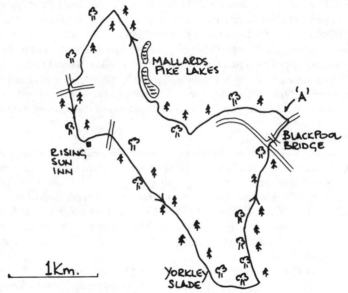

Begin by traversing the western shore of the lake near **Mallards Pike** to its northern end (there is a further smaller lake, the two being divided by an embankment). Turn left for a few yards to a T-junction, where you should turn right and head north. The broad track crosses another, and continues just west of north to another cross where a small tree stump bears the figure '3'. Turn left for ¹/₄ mile to another junction, this time marked with a '2' but keep straight over (actually veering slightly left). Follow this broad track until it reaches a public road. There is a gate with a stile beside it and a rectangular stone bearing an inscription. Turn left down the road for a few yards to its junction with the B4431 then keep straight on in line, entering the trees and taking the central (and most prominent) of three paths. There is a small car park and picnic site here.

After 200 yards through beeches, where the main track swings right, bear slightly left, still on a prominent track. In a similar distance this track swings right but you keep straight on between fir trees. After a few yards take the middle path of three through dense conifers. Light is much reduced here but soon you emerge from the forest right by the Rising Sun pub. Bear left down the metalled drive to a road. Cross this and bear right on the obvious track in a south-east direction. Descending slightly then levelling out, this part of the route can be muddy after rain. After $^1/_4$ mile the track starts to rise and climbs for over $^1/_2$ mile. Over this section there is a line of electric posts alongside the path. Follow this line of posts as the way traverses the edge of woodland and the houses of Yorkley Slade appear to the right.

Cross a stile in a wire fence and soon a junction of several tracks is reached. To the left two stiles can be seen. Cross the second and proceed with a plantation of larch trees to your left. Two cross-tracks (the second quite wide), are passed as you start to descend. The path steepens: at the next cross-path turn left. After a few yards ignore a divergent track that slants rightwards; your path, quite narrow, advances northwards and, after rather more than $^1/_2$ mile, joins a much wider track. Keeping in the same line you soon descend to the B4431 at its junction with the road to Soudley. Straight ahead can be seen **Blackpool Bridge**, originally built for a railway. As you advance under the bridge and on for 100 yards, an exposed portion of an ancient road can be seen to the left. Walking on up the road for a further 200 yards you will come to a gate on the left with a stile alongside it. Cross the stile and advance a short distance to where a path comes in on the right. From here, maintain direction on the broad track that rises and falls as it crosses the hillside. (You will be aware of the road not far to the left.) In little more than 1 mile turn right at a T-junction. Soon Mallards Pike Lake can be seen to your left and a path round its southern end leads back to the car park.

POINTS OF INTEREST:
Mallards Pike – This mini beauty spot was created by the Forestry Commission in 1982.
Blackpool Bridge – The section of old road about 100 yards north-east of Blackpool Bridge was thought for many years to be Roman. It is now believed to date from medieval times.

REFRESHMENTS:
The Rising Sun Inn, Moseley Green (tel no: 0594 562008). Bar meals available at a pub in a real forest setting.

Walk 73 NORTH NIBLEY AND STINCHOMBE HILL 6³/₄m (10.5km)

Maps: OS Sheets Landranger 162; Pathfinder ST 69/79.

A reasonably strenuous walk with some steep climbs, but with beautiful views.

Start: The village of North Nibley.

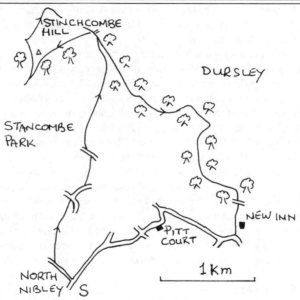

Take the road towards the **North Nibley** Church. Pass the Post Office and walk down the lane to your right at the small island with the large oak tree. This soon becomes a path meandering down to the main road. Notice the old gateway half-way down the path inscribed N M M H S P N C ANNO DNE 1607, part of an old estate, long since vanished. Be extremely cautious crossing the road at its bend and continue straight over and down towards some mill cottages with ponds. Follow the lane around and take the footpath up to the left, clearly marked by yellow arrows. The arrows take you upwards and over two fields to a gate emerging on the lane to **Stancombe Park**. Cross the stile opposite into a large field with views across to Stancombe House, and walk round to the edge of the woods. Go over a stile then down and up a series of steps to a track. Turn right and continue uphill until the path emerges on to Stinchcombe Hill's golf course.

Bear left towards the car park and follow the edge of the hill round to Drakestone Point. Keep to the footpaths at all times and beware of low-flying golf balls! The path continues round to a viewfinder and hut and eventually cuts across the top of the hill and back along the lane past the car park and club house. Turn left down the junction near 'Broadway' and almost immediately right into the woods above Dursley. At the first fork go left and at the second go right. Continue walking to a small clearing, taking the second track left and then right with the blue arrows. At a larger junction of woodland tracks, ignore the arrows and bear right, ultimately arriving at a lane. Turn left here, pass the small turn off to the right and keep straight on for approximately $^1/_4$ mile, taking the second track to the right down to an old shed. Continue down through the woods and round a sharp right-hand bend emerging finally at the New Inn. Leaving the pub, continue down the lane, bearing right all the way. At a small road island turn left and up the hill to Pitt Court. At a second island bear right on a road that will bring you, after $^1/_2$ mile, back to North Nibley.

POINTS OF INTEREST:

North Nibley – Reputed to have been the home of William Tyndale who translated the Bible from German into English. The monument (111ft high) on the hill above commemorates him. The keys for access to the monument may be obtained from the village shop.

Stancombe Park – Built around 1840, the house was once owned by a Miss Purnell who married the Rev. David Edwards, vicar of North Nibley. He created the romantic gardens hidden in trees below the house. It is reputed that he fell in love with a gypsy girl, and that the paths of the gardens were made especially narrow so that their love-makings should not be discovered by the over-large Miss Purnell!

REFRESHMENTS:

The Black Horse, North Nibley (tel no: 0453 46841).
The New Inn, Waterley Bottom (tel no: 0453 3659).

Maps: OS Sheets Landranger 162; Pathfinder SO 80/90.

A very hilly walk.

Start: At 858061, in Stroud at the junction of Folly Lane and Peghouse Rise.

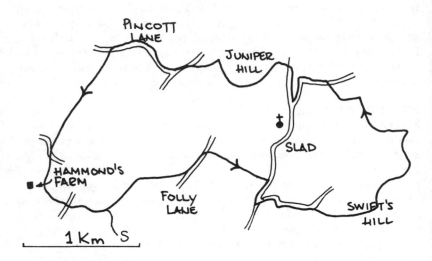

Continue along Folly Lane and opposite Wickridge Farm entrance turn left over a stile to climb the first field by the left boundary, the second field by the right boundary, and the third field by the left boundary. Ascend the lane on the right and cross the field at the top by the left boundary. Turn left along the road for 300 yards. At Worgan's Wood turn right and descend through two fields by the left boundary, then go by the right boundary down a lane and footpath to Slad Road (B4070). Turn right for 300 yards, then left down Elcombe Road for $1/_2$ mile, ascending left at the junction to a cattle grid. Climb Swift's Hill on the right, then go by the left boundary to steps to a stile on the left, and by the right boundary across Trantershill Plantation. After a cart-track, go by the left boundary up to the right boundary in the long field until you meet the cart-track to Catswood Lane.

Turn left down the road for 300 yards, and directly into Catswood at the road bends. Descending past a right fork, turn left at a track junction, and go by the left boundary along an elevated footpath to a footpath junction. Turn right, and keep the left boundary to Steanbridge. Turn left and climb the road, veering left, through **Slad** village to the Woolpack Inn. From the pub turn right along the B4070 to the War Memorial. Climb the bridleway on the left beside the wood, and directly over the top. At the field's end turn immediately left down a footpath through the wood to Wick Street. Turn left and in 100 yards right, down Pincott Lane. Go left between Wick Street and Primrose Cottages down a cart-track and (by left boundary) through two fields to a road. Turn left for 60 yards, then right, and go by the right boundary through two fields. At Hammonds Farm turn left along the drive, cross Wick Street, and go up the lane by 'Forty Acres' to the third field from the start. From here retrace your steps to Folly Lane.

POINTS OF INTEREST:
Slad – Laurie Lee grew up in the village and immortalised it in his book *Cider With Rosie*. Just before the junction of the village road with the B4070 there is a green lane which leads to Rose Cottage, the author's childhood home. There are also steps down to it from the B4070.

Fly orchids can be found on Swift's Hill during the month of June.

REFRESHMENTS:
The Woolpack Inn, Slad (tel no: 0452 813429).

Walk 75   BROCKWEIR TO BIGSWEIR   7m (11km)

Maps: OS Sheets Landranger 162; Outdoor Leisure 14.

*A walk along variations of the Offa's Dyke Footpath and including
a section of river bank.*

Start: In Gwent, at 538007, the 'Old Station' car park near
Tintern.

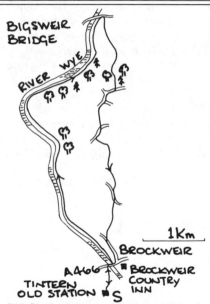

Go north from the **Old Station** along a broad track (the former railway) passing
children's play apparatus. After $^1/_4$ mile you will come to the road (stile) that crosses
the river over Brockweir Bridge. Cross the bridge and immediately turn left. A metalled
roadway gives way to a concrete path: then a stile is followed by 1 mile of grassy river
bank with a stile near half-way. Gates are positioned at both ends of a short wooded
section, then after more grassy river bank the route merges with a broad track
converging from the right, where another wood is encountered. Where the track leaves
the trees, go over a stile on the left and walk the last $^1/_2$ mile of river bank to Bigsweir
Bridge.

    Climb over a stile and turn right along the A466 for 30 yards then turn right again on a broad stony track. Fork right after a few yards and advance to a cattle grid, where you walk left across a field. Go past an electricity pole and aim for a small tree in midfield. Keep on in line, stepping over a low wire fence (which may be a temporary feature). Head just right of the top corner of the field and a stile will become evident. Climb over this, near a stricken sweet chestnut tree, and go up and slightly left of straight, across the next field. (A faint but visible track will take you too far left.) On the far side go over a stile into a wood but after a few yards bear left and follow a steep path through the trees. Near the forestry's upper edge go right then left between walls. Turn right along a metalled road but bear left at a house named 'Sittingreen'. Turn right at the next junction on a road that soon becomes a stony track. Go right along a metalled road until 60 yards beyond 'Denehurst', you can climb over a stile on the left. Walk up the side of a field to a pair of stiles then bear slightly right diagonally across a field to a shed. Bear left along a track for a few yards then turn right down a track between walls and after 150 yards bear right again. Where this track meets the public road bear left and follow the lane down until it bends left. Here, leave the **Offa's Dyke Footpath** route by taking the narrow lane going slightly right of straight and where this bends sharply right, go left down a track. Keep in approximately the same line going to the right of a white house and almost straight over a junction below it. At the next road bear left to Brockweir. Turn right and cross the Wye Bridge going left over the stile on the other side, and walking back to the car park.

POINTS OF INTEREST:
Tintern Old Station–Served the now dismantled railway that once traversed the lower Wye Valley. Various features are preserved, including the signal box which houses interesting displays. There are toilets, car park, a café and a picnic site here.
Offa's Dyke Footpath – Stretching from North Wales to the Severn, this was built by Offa, King of Saxon Mercia. Parts of the old earthworks can be seen in several places.

REFRESHMENTS:
Tintern Station café (tel no: 0291 689566). Open during the summer months.
Brockweir Country Inn (tel no: 0291 689548). Bar food available.

Maps: OS Sheets Landranger 162; Pathfinder ST 88/99.

A very pleasant and interesting walk penetrating a remote area south of Nailsworth.

Start: The Nailsworth car park just off the A46.

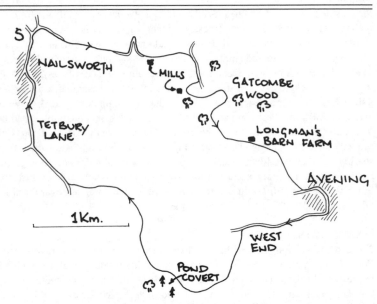

Go down to the clock tower and cross over to pass in front of the Midland Bank. Go over the cattle grid and turn right by the Motor Co. into Pensile Road. Stay on this road for about 1 mile and, after passing through a beech wood, you come to Iron Mills Common. At the T-junction take the Minchinhampton road left and in 100 yards take the right turn, signposted 'Longford Mill ¹/₄ mile'. Go between the mill buildings at the bottom of the descent and continue on to the Avening-Nailsworth road. Turn left towards Avening. **Gatcombe Park** can be seen across the valley to the left. Proceed on this road for 400 yards round Boathouse Corner with a lovely view of Longfords Lake to the left. Just past this bend look for a bridleway on the right up into a wood. In 150 yards emerge from the wood and leave the track by the first field gate on the left. Follow the hedge on the right and the track up the field to the top and pass through another gate. Turn left and pass along the top side of a farm, through a gate and straight across two fields to another gate.

Pass through the gate and walk on a path between hedges which leads to a better track that you follow down to Avening. Reaching the main road go right, passing a garage, and then turn right up New Inn Lane by Gibbons Restaurant. Continue up the hill, turn right into Point Lane, passing Esther's Cottage. Stay on this road through West End, passing a seat on the left, and go on down to the stream. Take the left fork towards the fields, go over a double stile and follow a stream descending from the left. Follow this stream up the valley, through a gate and, ignoring the bridge and gate left, go on straight ahead through another gate to arrive at the bottom of a wood. Pass this wood which is on your left and notice the pond over the wall where ducks, and even a heron, might be seen. Ignore the gate at the end of the wood and walk on up the valley to the next gate in a facing stone wall. Follow the stone wall on your left and, staying in the valley bottom, go up the field which has a lot of scrub. Walk below trees to a gateway, pass through and enter another field. In 150 yards go over a stile in the corner and, following the same wall, cross another field and over a stone stile.

Now follow the track across the field but be sure you go over a stone stile in the left corner. Cross into another field with a hedge on the left which leads to a gate giving access to a lane. Go straight ahead and after 25 yards turn right into another lane. This is Tetbury Lane and will take you down to the A46. Turn right and go down into **Nailsworth**.

POINTS OF INTEREST:

Gatcombe Park – The home of the Princess Royal can be seen on the left across the valley from the fields before Avening. You can also see the cross-country obstacles for the annual horse trials.

Nailsworth – A busy town straddling the A46 where there are many inns and cafés for the weary walker.

REFRESHMENTS:

Numerous in Nailsworth.

Walk 77   CENTRAL DEAN FOREST   7m (11km)

Maps: OS Sheets Landranger 162; Outdoor Leisure 14.

An undulating walk almost entirely through mixed forest.

Start: At 615120, the Forestry Commission site at Beechenhurst.

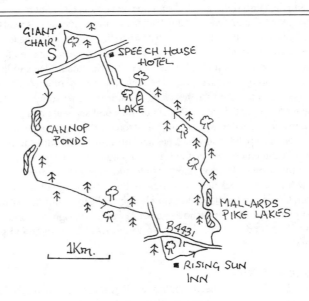

Return to the main road, turn right and walk down it for 300 yards before turning left on to a broad forestry road. After another 600 yards the most northerly of Cannop Ponds can be seen to the right. Walk round the northern end and follow the western shore to the southern end, where you go left. Cross the stream joining the two ponds and shortly bear right. It is now possible to follow a waymarked path (yellow arrows) along the east side of the southern pond. At the south-east corner move left to cross the main track (the former course of a railway) and look for a junction where two paths come in from the east. The more northerly comes by way of a stile. Ignore this, and take the more southerly. Keep in the same line over all junctions until a road is reached by a stile. The entrance to the New Fancy site (viewpoint, car park and picnic site) can be seen to the left but turn right along the road to its junction with the B4431.

   Keep straight on in line, entering the trees and taking the central (and most prominent) of three paths. There is a small car park and picnic site here. After 200 yards through beeches, where the main track swings right, bear slightly left but still on a prominent track. In a similar distance this track swings right but you keep straight on between fir trees. After a few yards take the middle path of three, south-east for 75 yards, to reach the Rising Sun. Bear left down the metalled drive to a public road. Cross this and in a few yards bear left (north-east) to go between oak trees. The track can just be made out and reaches the B4431 by the direction board to Mallards Pike. Turn right down the road for 100 yards then left into the Mallards Pike site (see Walk 72). Follow the footpath round the southern end of the first lake and then follow the eastern shore. At the top of the first lake, go left to pass between the lakes and then turn right on to a broad forestry track. Take the right fork at the next junction. After 200 yards and immediately after crossing a stream, turn left on to a small, waymarked, path. This path meanders up through trees to a junction with another broad track, where you bear right. After 200 yards turn left (the waymarking ends here) and follow a straight forestry track for almost 1 mile. Turn left where Speech House Lake can be seen through the trees. Cross the footbridge at the lake's outlet and carry on, but turn right just before a stile. At a junction bear left through a gate and, shortly, right along a public road. The Speech House Hotel (see Walk 46) can be seen ahead. Walk up to it and cross the B4226.

There is a four-way finger post here, but go 30 yards right to a stone obelisk and take the path from there. Go over a stile, down a slope and turn left along a well-defined track. As you leave the trees the Giant Chair, an item on the Forestry Commissions Sculpture Trail, can be seen ahead. Go to it (a fine viewpoint) then turn sharp left and follow the path back to Beechenhurst.

REFRESHMENTS:
The Rising Sun, Moseley Green (tel no: 0594 562008). Bar meals available at a pub in a real forest setting.
The Speech House Hotel (tel no: 0594 22607). Bar meals available or full restaurant service, also afternoon teas.
Beechenhurst Forestry Commission Site. Drinks and snacks available.

Walk 78   STAUNTON AND REDBROOK $7^3/_4$m (12.5km)

Maps: OS Sheets Landranger 162; Outdoor Leisure 14.

*A walk partly through woodland and partly through pleasant
meadowland.*

Start: At 539124, at a lay-by on the north side of the A4136 about
$^1/_2$ mile west from Staunton.

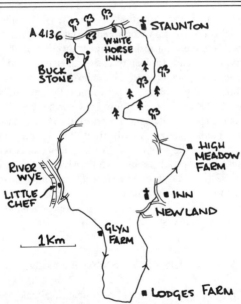

Opposite the upper end of the lay-by, a path climbs steeply through woodland. Walk
up it and go straight over a cross-track. Well-defined at first, the path becomes a little
indistinct but persevere and go through a gap in a wall to a T-junction. If you want to
visit the Buck Stone (see Walk 49), turn left here. Otherwise, turn right, downhill, and
shortly go right; then left, near a red-shingled house. Cross a road and go down to a
T-junction. Go right, passing Knockalls Lodge, then follow yellow arrows down to a
road where you bear right towards Redbrook. Just before reaching a bridge, bear left
(marked 'Offa's Dyke Path') on a path and after 200 yards emerge on to the A466. Turn
left and walk along the road to a petrol station, at the far end of which go left, then right
up some concrete steps. Cross the tarmac road at the top and ascend a narrow lane for

perhaps 80 yards. Go left over a stile and climb the steep field above. Cross another stile and, just beyond a third, turn left down a stony track. Where this track bends sharply left, head straight on. Go through a gate, then another, and descend gradually to Glyn Farm and another gate.

Now walk up the valley bottom. Where the track bends right towards a house, go straight ahead through a gate. When a second house appears ahead, go through a gate and take the track to the left of the building. Just beyond, bear left on a stony track and follow this to **Newland**. As you enter the village turn right then left up a steep lane. At the top bear right, across the churchyard, emerging opposite the Ostrich pub. Turn left for 200 yards then go right, through a gate and over a stile to the left. Walk across the field to a kissing gate. Go over the track beyond and climb another stile. Now walk across the next field to a stile. Keeping in the same line, cross to a stile in the right-hand boundary of the next field and on to yet another stile in the opposite fence. Now aim for a building (High Meadow Farm), but just before it turn left and walk down the fence to a stile (to comply with the Right of Way). Keep on across the following field to a gate. Cross the public road and walk along the road opposite for 40 yards, then bear right through a gate.

Make for a stile near the top left-hand corner of the field beyond, then turn left on a path through the forestry. At a junction look for a path between the two well-defined forestry tracks. Bear right after 200 yards and go on for 600 yards to a broad forestry road, where you bear left. At a four-way junction bear left on a greenish track that eventually becomes more stony. Proceed in the same line to the main road almost opposite Staunton church. Go left along a minor road then turn right at the village shop back to the main road (A4136). Turn left and walk the $^1/_2$ mile back to the lay-by.

POINTS OF INTEREST:
Newland – The large village church is known as the 'Cathedral of the Forest', and possesses some fine monuments.

REFRESHMENTS:
The Little Chef, Redbrook (tel no: 0600 3251).
The Ostrich, Newland (tel no: 0594 33260). Bar meals, afternoon teas.
The White Horse Inn, Staunton (tel no: 0594 33387). Bar meals.

Walk 79   DEAN FOREST AND STAPLE EDGE   8¹/₂m (13km)

Maps: OS Sheets Landranger 162; Outdoor Leisure 14.

An undulating walk almost entirely through mixed forest.

Start: At 637092, the car park at Mallards Pike.

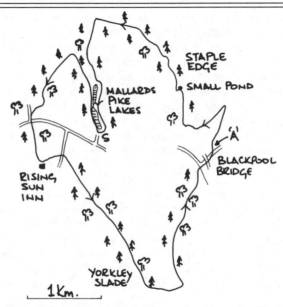

The first part of the walk is identical to Walk 72 up to the point – after Blackpool Bridge (see Walk 72) – where the path comes in on the right.

Take the path to the right and in little more than 100 yards a stile can be seen to the right. Cross this and follow the path until it joins a broad track at an oblique angle. Turn sharply left. The route is now marked by yellow arrows. (Care should be taken since some of the arrows are not easily seen and at one point another waymarked route crosses yours.) Follow the broad track and shortly cross another stile alongside a gateway. The way now swings more and more right until you are walking northward. Eventually the track starts to swing left in a much tighter bend. A small pond can be seen at the outer edge. Having almost negotiated the bend turn sharply right up a slope. Bearing first left then right on narrow paths you come to a broader track, where you turn left. Soon Staple End bungalows can be seen in a clearing, the route being directed

166

along the western boundary (with the bungalows to your right). Here, the other waymarked route is encountered again, crossing at right angles. You should go straight across the junction, bearing slightly left and soon descending.

Two junctions are passed before a stream is crossed by a footbridge, and yet another junction is passed before you turn left. This track is fairly well defined but where it swings right after some 200 yards take a lesser path to the left. The path meanders downwards until it gives on to a wider track where you turn right. Almost immediately leave the wider track on its left and wind between huge conifers, crossing a stream several times by means of log bridges. You are now on the eastern shore of the more northerly, and smaller, of the two Mallards Pike lakes (see Walk 72). At an embankment between the lakes keep to the eastern side of the larger lake and walk round the southern end, back to the car park.

REFRESHMENTS:
The Rising Sun Inn, Moseley Green (tel no: 0594 562008).

Walk 80   STANDISH AND STOCKEND   8½m (13.5km)

Maps: OS Sheets Landranger 162; Pathfinder SO 80/90.

A hilly figure-of-eight walk.

Start: At 831086, the National Trust's Shortwood car park.

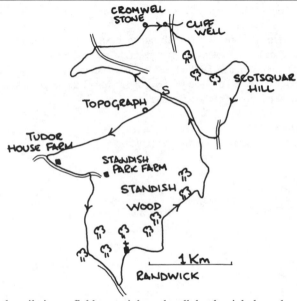

Go over the stile into a field, turn right and walk by the right boundary following the Cotswold Way (waymarked with yellow arrow and white spot) to Haresfield Beacon. At the Beacon trig. point turn sharp right and follow the Cotswold Way down to the road and on through the wood opposite the farm past the **Cromwell Stone** to **Cliff Well**. Descend the drive of Tump Farm to a stile on the right. Keep by the left boundary in the first field, contour through the centre of the next and continue under Halliday Wood, keeping by the right boundary in the last field to the drive of Randall's Farm.

Opposite the next house on the left, climb the field and veer left up through the copse to the top left corner. Turn right along the footpath to the bridleway (Cotswold Way) and 50 paces along to the right ascend a footpath to the road at the top of Scotsquar Wood. Cross the field opposite diagonally left to right (SSW) to Stoneridge Farm. At the 'Bird in Hand' fork right along the Randwick road, enter the first field on the right opposite Birch House and hold the left boundary to the car park (the starting point).

To complete the figure-of-eight go over the stile again but this time follow the Cotswold Way to the **Topograph**. Continue directly down a cart-track to a stile on the right. Pass behind pens and descend the path through the centre of fields to a barn in the bottom right corner, and through the farmyard to the road. Turn left past 'Martins' for $^1/_2$ mile to Standish Park Farm. Ascend a cart-track on the right between barns through a field, then go via the right gate into a hollow lane, and directly forward at junctions. Before the path enters a field at a cross-tracks, ascend left around a quarry (SE). The **Randwick Ash** viewpoint is at the next cross-tracks.

Descend the road, turn left by a hut along a footpath by the right boundary to St John the Baptist Church, Randwick. Follow the path through the churchyard and the school playground to the road. Ascend the footpath opposite left. Turn left at the first junction, cross the second junction (left for Vine Tree Inn), then go left to a stile into a field, and right in the field by the right boundary over two stiles. Ascend left by the left boundary to the road. Turn immediately right along the 'No Through Road', and after the horseshoe bend, before a cottage on the left, climb Ruscombe Wood. Take two stiles by the left boundary to the road. Keep the left boundary in Standish Wood and then the right fork on to the Cotswold Way and back to the car park.

POINTS OF INTEREST:

Cromwell Stone – Commemorates Oliver Cromwell's Siege of Gloucester and is dated 10 August to 5 September 1643. As a campsite it afforded an excellent prospect of the city. The cathedral can be seen to the left of Robinswood Hill.

Cliff Well – Stands beside Cliffwell House. Unfortunately it has recently been concreted in and you need imagination when reading the inscription above it. However, it is an impressive and interesting building.

The Topograph – Near the car park, it is one of the best in Britain.

Randwick Ash is a local viewpoint.

REFRESHMENTS:

The Vine Tree Inn, Randwick (tel no: 04536 3748).

Walk 81   HARESCOMBE AND HARESFIELD   9m (14.5km)

Maps: OS Sheets Landranger 162; Pathfinder SO 80/90 & 81/91.
A mostly level walk in a quiet rural corner of the Severn Plain.
Start: At 847097, near the church in Edge.

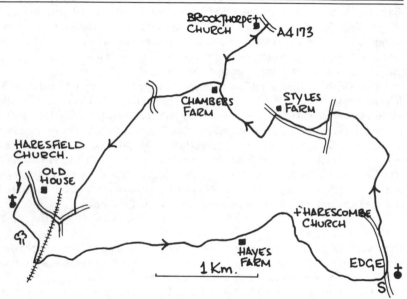

Walk to the A4173 via the short link road before Edge church. Cross over, turn left and at the next bus stop turn right into a driveway, veering left and up some steps. At the top hold the left boundary to the field entrance then the right boundary to the field corner. Turn left, keeping the right boundary through three fields and veering left to a gate. Descend to the hedge corner and the A4173. Turn left. Cross the road near the next gate, climb a fence into the field corner and head diagonally to the gate. Turn right along the road and then left opposite **Styles Farm**. Go across the field to the gate near the left corner. Turn right and follow Daniel's Brook to the road and cross the opposite field to a footbridge on the right. Go by the left boundary over a stile, through a gate on the left, and over a field to the road. To visit **Brookthorpe Church** cross to the jutting hedge corner and on to a gate, then veer right across three fields. Return to the road.

Take the stile opposite, left, by Chambers Farm, and walk through the centre of the field towards **Haresfield Church** in the distance (west) to the gate. Hold the left boundary through the next two fields, over a footbridge and a stile to the road. Cross the following four fields, well away from the right boundary. Turn right along Gloucester Road to the church (access on the left). South of the church, a footpath across a field keeps left of the copse, and goes directly over the next field to the road. Turn right, then left over the railway to the pub.

Continue past the Post Office, turn right along the road, then left into the field. Veer right in the second field, turn right in the third to a footbridge and go diagonally to the right corner in the fourth. Go right in the fifth field, left to the corner of the sixth, rising to the top right corner by a copse. Go over a stile and through a gate on the left. Continue (east) near the left boundary directly over three fields, contouring (or climbing) small hills, and pass through Hayes Farm to a road.

Along the road opposite, by Stocks Farm, a path descends the field on the left to the road to **Harescombe Church**. At the far end of the graveyard climb a stile to the right of the kissing gate and keep the right boundary before crossing the second field to a road. Turn left, and, shortly, right through a gate. Climb diagonally left towards a cottage on the road, and up two fields opposite to the road. Turn left and either ascend to **Edge Church**, if you wish, or go left into the field after Hill House Farm. Climb to the far top corner and hug the left boundary to the next stile. Go over and climb the field, right and back to the A4173 and the start point.

POINTS OF INTEREST:

Brookthorpe Church – St Swithun's has a small baroque chamber organ.

Haresfield Church – St Peter's is Norman and Medieval. Keys are available from 8 Merryfields.

Harescombe Church – St John the Baptist has a massive 13th-century double bell-turret.

Edge Church – St John the Baptist is rock-faced early Victorian. The first set of steps has passing places for ladies in crinolines.

Styles Farm – Sells cider from the wood. Bring your own bottle!

REFRESHMENTS:

The Beacon Hotel, Haresfield (tel no: 0452 728884).

Walk 82   SELSLEY AND NYMPSFIELD   9m (14.5km)

Maps: OS Sheets Landranger 162; Pathfinder SO 80/90 &60/70.
A hilly walk, rough underfoot but challenging, varied and scenic.
Start: At 829027, near the portaloo on Selsley Common.

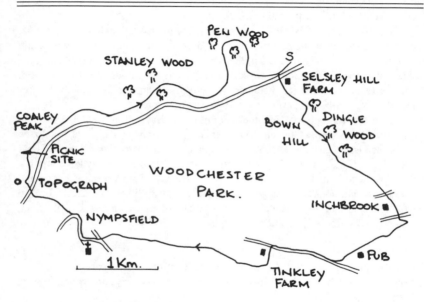

From the portaloo (open Easter to October!) walk beside the B4066 towards Dursley and just before the cattle grid turn left into the footpath signposted 'Inchbrook'. Following the line of the drive, cross it and walk by the wall on the left in the second field. Turn left through the field gate and keep by the left boundary over two fields to a stone stile. Walk by telegraph poles, veering left at the third, and keep the same direction over the next two fields to the bottom right corner and a copse path. Cross the cart-track (entrance to Woodchester Park) and descend two fields to the footbridge to Inchbrook. Cross by the warehouse to steps uphill through the copse and two fields. Climb the road, veer left at the junction, then right opposite the signpost 'Windsoredge Lane' into the footpath ahead. You can also start this walk from Coaley Peak car park and picnic site, and you will reach the Jovial Foresters at lunch-time by continuing down Windsoredge Lane and turning right at the T-junction.

To continue, keep the right-hand boundary via the road to the footpath on the right leading to a stile into a field and across to a stone stile. Cross the next field diagonally and take the left-hand field gate at the corner. Continue across Wood Farm drive to a stile in the hedge, and climb the next field to a stile to a road. Turn right for $^{1}/_{2}$ mile to Tinkley Farm, then left and left again through farm buildings to a field. Veer right and swing right to hold the right-hand boundary through two long fields. Cross a scramble track field and head toward Nympsfield (west) now visible on the skyline, before descending to a hollow and a footbridge over Miry Brook. The right-hand boundary through the next two fields leads you round to a pedestrian gate by power lines. At the road turn right then left up to St. Margaret's Church and the Rose and Crown.

Go left at the crossroads beyond the pub to a footpath on the right, and cross two fields to the B4066. Over the road the left-hand boundary leads to the Cotswold Way (waymarked with yellow arrow and white spot), and the **Frocester Hill Topograph.**

Continue along the Cotswold Way through Coaley Peak car park and picnic site, Buckholt Wood, Woodside Farm fields, and Stanley Wood for $2^{1}/_{2}$ miles. Approximately 30 paces after the County Council footpath sign in Penn Wood where the Cotswold Way drops down left by a building, turn right and climb to the top, where a path veers off left (to avoid road walking) back to Selsley Common.

POINTS OF INTEREST:
Frocester Hill Topograph – An excellent viewpoint. Nearby the Cotswold Way passes a prehistoric burial ground in the Coaley Peak site.
At the right time of the year you can find good mushrooms and puffballs in the two fields before the scramble track field.

REFRESHMENTS:
The Jovial Foresters (tel no: 045383 2254).
The Rose and Crown (tel no: 0453 860240).

Walk 83   THE WYE VALLEY, BROCKWEIR   9m (14.5km)

Maps: OS Sheets Landranger 162; Outdoor Leisure 14.

A walk mostly through woodland and partly along the river bank.

Start: At 538007, the 'Old Station' car park near Tintern.

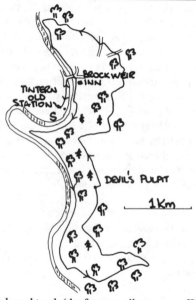

Go north along a broad track (the former railway – see Walk 75) passing a children's playground. After ¼ mile you reach Brockweir Bridge. Cross it and turn right just past Brockweir Country Inn. After 30 yards go right again past Brookside Cottage. Pass the Moravian Church, right, and go on to cross a stile into a field. Go along the river bank for about 300 yards then turn left (yellow arrow) to cross the field and go up a bank to a stile. Go over and turn right on a broad track and shortly go through a gate to enter a wood. Follow the track as it gains height with the river below, to the right. When the track begins to descend you will see the river to your left, the Wye having executed a 180 degree bend. The track is stepped in places and soon leads to a broad, level track.

Turn left along the track and in less than ¼ mile you will see to your left the entrance to a tunnel, now disused. For the next 1½ miles you will be walking along the old railway. At a clearing, take an obvious track going leftward and up. Bear right at a T-junction, ignoring arrows to the left. After 300 yards, fork left, uphill through dense woodland. In about $^1/_2$ mile the path bends right on to a forestry road. Turn left and walk uphill to meet the Offa's Dyke Path (waymarked with white acorns – see Walk 75). Turn left up steps and follow the path through woodland. After almost 1 mile go right at a junction of paths and walk with steep downward slopes to the left. A rock just below the path offers good views towards Tintern Abbey. A little way beyond, there is a memorial seat to Chris Pugh, a former Wye Valley Warden. Some 250 yards on look for the **Devil's Pulpit** down to the left, another fine viewpoint.

At another junction go left towards 'Monmouth'. At a further signpost go on and after a descent go straight over a cross-track and between metal posts (indistinct arrow on large stone). A little way on, cross a stile with an information board nearby. The woodland is now behind and the way contours for a short distance until an arrow on a large log indicates that you should descend leftwards across a field to a post in the centre and on in the same line to the other side. Turn right along the hedge, then left through a gate to descend between fences to another signpost. Take the path signposted 'Hudnalls', keeping to the right of a grassy mound and the line of trees below. In the left-hand bottom corner of the field a stile is followed by a footbridge. Bear left through the wood to where a stile gives access to a road. On the other side, and slightly to the right, go along a track, keeping straight on at a junction, then crossing a footbridge to another lane. Go left for a few yards then sharply right on a track. After 200 yards go left on a metalled lane, forking left by Tump Cottage. After three bends a house appears ahead. A kissing gate to the left allows you to cross a field diagonally to another kissing gate below the house. Walk along a level path for 100 yards then turn left down through a delightful wood. Two stone stiles are crossed before the path arrives at a road, where you turn left. Walk along the road for some 200 yards and, just after passing a cottage on the left, look for a metal stile on the right. Go over it and another, then diagonally across the field to yet another. Go over this and the next and descend to the river bank. Brockweir Bridge is now in sight downriver, so go towards it, crossing a stile on the way. Cross the bridge to the stile on the left and retrace your steps back to the car park.

POINTS OF INTEREST:
Devil's Pulpit – A prominent rock that overlooks the Wye Valley almost opposite Tintern Abbey. Legend has it that from it the Devil preached to the monks in the abbey grounds, trying to entice them from their work.

REFRESHMENTS:
Tintern Station café . Open during the summer months.

Walk 84   CRANHAM AND COOPER'S HILL $9^3/_4$m (15.5km)

Maps: OS Sheets Landranger 162 & 163; Pathfinder SO 81/91.

An undulating walk largely through or along the edge of woodland.

Start: At 892131, by a small clearing $^1/_4$ mile west of Cranham.

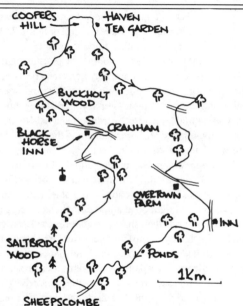

Follow a track, waymarked by yellow arrows with red bases, as it rises north-west through Buckholt Wood. Crossing a road, the track continues to rise until, levelling out, it merges with the Cotswold Way which forms the route for the next 3 miles. This part is waymarked by yellow/red arrows with white dots. Follow the Way until it emerges on to the open space at the top of **Cooper's Hill**.

A steep track to the left of the cheese-rolling slope takes you to a lower level where the Cotswold Way resumes its eastern progress. About $1^1/_2$ miles beyond Haven Café a large clearing is reached. Leave the Way here on a track that turns sharply right and climbs to a road. Cross this and almost immediately bear left to follow the boundary of what was once the Cotswold Sanatorium. Pass the last building on the right, veer slightly left and negotiate a tight right-hand bend. Ignore a right-hand branch and after 200 yards bear right. At the edge of the trees bear right again to a road.

Turn left and walk along the road for 300 yards, then bear right through Overtown Farm. Keeping to the left of all buildings go through the gate on the far side. Go across a large field, aiming slightly left of a distant house. No path is discernible at first, although it is possible further over to pick out a slight furrow. At the field's far corner go through a gate and bear right along a road for 200 yards. Turn right at an obvious entrance and go through two gates in quick succession. The second one is labelled 'Bridleway to Far End' in blue paint and for the next $1\frac{1}{2}$ miles the route is waymarked with blue arrows. The bridleway is the middle track at the next two junctions. Two small ponds are passed to the left and after another $\frac{1}{4}$ mile the track nears the edge of the wood. Bear left at the next two junctions to keep near the edge of the trees and soon you will reach a macadam road at Far End (the blue arrows cease here).

Go along the road for 200 yards, then bear right up a stony track signposted 'Sheepscombe Cricket Club'. The track climbs and starts to veer right (ignore a sharper right turn to a gate). Shortly the cricket field can be seen through trees to the right. A National Trust sign is passed as the walker enters 'Lords Wood'. At another National Trust sign leave the wood and at the next junction bear slightly right to go along the edge of Saltridge Wood. At the end of the trees go through a gate and ahead to another gate. Through this, look for a stile slightly to the left and only a few yards away. Climb over the stile and head towards the buildings of Overtown. Negotiate a kissing gate, then go downhill at an acute angle to the fence heading for a small footbridge. Cross this and almost immediately jump over another stream. Go through a small gate and bear left down the slope keeping near the fence. Ahead can be seen a gate giving access to a wood. The track ascends obliquely through the trees and emerges on to Cranham Common. Keep in the same line until a road is reached. Crossing the road, turn right and keep to the lower boundary of the common towards the village of **Cranham**. When you reach the Black Horse, go left down to the main street and bear left for the start.

POINTS OF INTEREST:

Cooper's Hill – Scene of cheese-rolling events held at Whitsuntide. Cheeses are rolled down a rough steep slope and pursued by daredevil competitors.

Cranham – The church, a little way from the village, has two pairs of shears carved high on the outside of the tower, a feature suggesting it was built by wool merchants.

REFRESHMENTS:

The Black Horse Inn, Cranham (tel no: 0452 812217).
The Butchers Arms, Sheepscombe (tel no: 0452 812113).
Haven Tea Garden, Cooper's Hill (tel no: 0452 863213).

Walk 85 RODBOROUGH AND MINCHINHAMPTON 10m (16km)

Maps: OS Sheets Landranger 162; Pathfinder SO 80/90 and ST 89/99.

An easy, mainly level elevated walk which is mostly mud free.
Start: At 833038, car park near Rodborough Fort campsite.

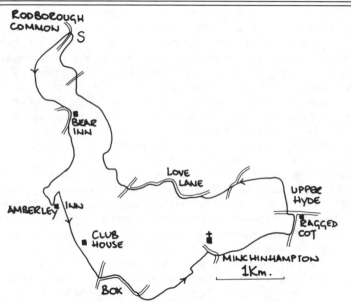

Head south-west towards the copse of dark trees (where there is a plaque commemorating Lord Baden-Powell), then veer left past the dew pond to a wall. Follow the track beside the wall to the Bear Inn. About 300 yards along St Chloe Road, turn left at Rambler Cottage on to a footpath. Keep to the right-hand boundary past Moor Court to Amberley Bakery and the Black Horse Inn. Turn left opposite the inn, then right (down), then left along to a footpath on the right, and left to the Amberley Inn.

At the crossroads take the Stroud road up to the Post Office. Turn right across the common. Pass the golf club to Halfway House, Box. When the road through Box turns left at the village end follow the cart-track for Longfords, turning left into a footpath in the second field and right, then first left, on reaching the road. Descend via the next signposted footpath to a field pond, and climb the next three fields by the left-hand boundaries to the top corner of the third. Cross Workhouse Lane into a walled path which leads to Friday Street and **Minchinhampton**.

The walk continues via Tobacconist Road. Pass through the farm and seek out stone stiles across six fields, ENE, veering east beside the wall through fields five and six. Turn left to the Ragged Cot, Hyde, then left and first right. As the road bends at Stud Farm, keep straight on along the footpath to the far left corner of the field. Veer left in the next field and follow the right-hand boundary via three stiles to the road. Cross over and continue past four more stiles and above Besbury Common to the next road. Turn left along Love Lane. Turn left at the road junction by a cattle grid, keep right at the crossroads, and continue into the cart-track by Laburnam Cottage. Walk across the common to the head of a busy dell, and after a cattle trough turn down in front of 'Commons Corner House' and veer right down road.

Keep left at the road junction, pass Bownham Park and go left at next junction to Winstones Ice Cream Company kiosk. Skirt round the top of the bushy dell ahead, cross road and turn towards a gate in the wall. Keeping this boundary on your left follow it round to the road over Rodborough Common. Turn right for the start.

POINTS OF INTEREST:
Minchinhampton – Has a Medieval Street Fair, usually on the first Saturday of September.
Rodborough Common – During the month of June keep a watchful eye out for bee orchid on the opposite side of the road to the car park.

REFRESHMENTS:
The Black Horse (tel no: 045387 2556).
The Amberley Inn (tel no: 045387 2565).
Halfway House (tel no: 045383 2631).
The Crown (tel no: 0453 882357).
The Coffee Bean (tel no: 0453 883382).
The Ragged Cot, Hyde (tel no: 0453 884643).

Walk 86   PAINSWICK AND SHEEPSCOMBE   10m (16km)

Maps: OS Sheets Landranger 162; Pathfinder SO 80/81.

A typical Cotswold walk – hills and woods, good views and pretty villages.

Start: At 865095, the car park, Stamages Lane, Painswick.

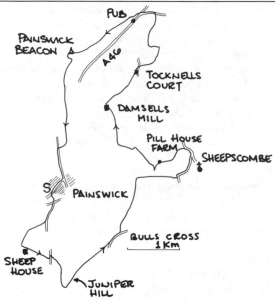

Descend Stamages Lane, **Painswick,** into Stepping Stone Lane, and take the footpath to the right by **Painswick Brook**. Cross the sluice and turn left by King's Mill House along a track which joins the lane to Sheephouse. Turn left up a footpath and continue directly to Wick Street. Turn left along the road and fork right three times to reach the top of Juniper Hill by a cart-track. At a T-junction turn left over a stile and cross the field with a wall on your left to a woodland track. Continue directly for $^3/_4$ mile to Bulls Cross (B4070).

Follow the Birdlip road to a finger post and turn left along a footpath. Turn right along a track and continue directly into a field and wood, keeping to the left boundary. On reaching the road, ascend right on a drive past Cockshoot House, entering the wood again. Keep to the lower part of the wood and about $^1/_2$ mile from Cockshoot you will find a stile and a footpath descending to the road junction with a sign 'Sheepscombe Village'. Descend past the church, turn left at the monument and descend and ascend to the Butchers Arms. Sixty yards on, take the footpath left between houses down one field and up two more with a hedge on the right, and across another field, with the hedge on the left, to Pill House Farm. Turn right through a gate and keep to the left boundary. Turn left at a gate and follow the track below the left boundary to a field gate. Descend through the centre of the field to a gate and stile in the bottom right-hand corner. You now follow the Painswick Brook for $1^1/_2$ miles, crossing it between Damsells Mill and Tocknells Court. Two roads are crossed and a third road reached at Suttons Mill. Here, turn left over a stile and ascend the field steeply to a road.

Turn left and right, and then right through a field gate. Contour to the house in a hollow and ascend to the gate and road. Cross the road and walk through the garden of 'Yewrick' to a stile and footpath. At the end of the footpath keep to the left boundary of the field until another footpath leads to the road. Turn left, cross the A46 and from here follow the Cotswold Way signs (yellow arrow and white spot). Diverge left from the wall, cross a road and continue to next road. Turn right on to a cart-track which leads to the trig. point on Painswick Beacon. Descend towards the quarry, but walk below it through a copse above the A46, diverging right on to a common and down to Painswick and the start of the walk.

POINTS OF INTEREST:
Painswick – Known as the Queen of the Cotswolds. The fine church with its many yew trees and iron stocks, and the many beautiful Cotswold houses are well worth exploring.
Painswick Brook – In the 17th century there were over two dozen mills along the brook.

REFRESHMENTS:
The Butchers Arms, Sheepscombe (tel no: 0452 812113).
The Royal William, Cranham (tel no: 0452 813650).
The Royal Oak, Painswick (tel no: 0452 813129).
The Cup House Restaurant, Painswick (tel no: 0452 812322).

Walks 87 and 88 VALE OF BERKELEY 11m(18km) or 14m(22km)

Maps: OS Sheets Landranger 162; Pathfinder ST 69/79.

Level walks through a deer park, farmland and the riverside.

Start: At 680984, near the Salutation Inn, Ham.

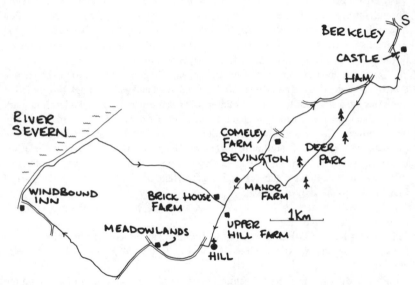

Walk south along the 'Stone' to a fork which is bisected by a footpath ascending a field to the deer park (see Walk 71). Walk along the crest of the ridge for $1^1/_2$ miles and turn right from the car park along the right boundary of a field, passing through a field gate and down a muddy cart-track. Turn left before Bevington Farm, keeping down by the right boundary and, after a gate, continue directly to the hedge corner and on to wooden rails. Follow the hedge to a lane. Turn right, then left into a field, veering right after the gate on to a footbridge. Follow the left boundary on to the road.

Seek out access directly across five fields to a drive below St Michael's Church, Hill. Descend right, turn left along the road for $^3/_4$ mile and then left into Oldbury Road opposite 'The Meadlands'. After a further $^1/_2$ mile take the second cart-track on the right for $^3/_4$ mile and then turn left to the road near a telephone box. Turn right and proceed along the road for $^3/_4$ mile to the Windbound Inn. With the River Severn on your left follow the embankment for 1$^1/_4$ miles and, at the first inlet, cross the bridge and turn right. Keep to the left boundary through long narrow fields and follow Stuckmoor Lane for 1$^1/_2$ miles to Brick House Farm. Cross the road into the lane opposite and then turn left over the footbridge.

Retrace the route to Bevington Farm, turning left into the farmyard and go along the drive to a gate where the road starts. Turn right into a field and cross two small fields to a stile. Then keep to the left boundary to reach a stile, a footbridge, a path and another stile. Keep by the left boundary to a gap in the hedge. Go through, and cross the next field diagonally to a footbridge. Cross another small field to a field gate. Enter the lane by Comeley Farm, turn left for 40 yards and turn right over a footbridge and wooden rails to go uphill steeply. Follow the right boundary to a field gate and fine view. Continue down the next field, keeping near the right boundary, to a field gate at a sharp bend in the road. Turn right for Ham and the start of the walk.

For the **longer walk**, start at Berkeley village (see Walk 71) and walk down High Street for $^1/_4$ mile. Take the footpath on the left signposted 'Woodford' and walk through the meadow to a bridge. Follow the stream south and at the next bridge turn right for Ham. Return the same way from Ham to Berkeley.

POINTS OF INTEREST:
There are excellent long views on both sides from the crest of the ridge in the deer park. Herds of deer can often be seen.

REFRESHMENTS:
The Windbound Inn, Shepperdine (tel no: 0454 414343).
The Salutation Inn, Ham (tel no: 0453 810284).

Walk 89   FRAMPTON-ON-SEVERN   12m (19km)

Maps: OS Sheets Landranger 162; Pathfinder SO 60/70.

A figure-of-eight walk beside dykes, ditches, river and canal.

Start: At 742067, Splatt Bridge south of Frampton-on-Severn.

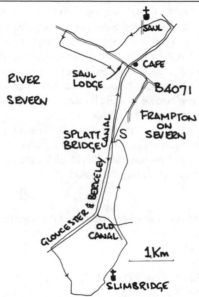

Cross Splatt Bridge, and turn right by the canal (see Walk 57), past two bridges to Junction Bridge House. Turn left over a stile behind a building, and after the third gate veer left to a footbridge in the field corner. Turn right, then veer right to St James of Saul church. Follow the footpath beside Alma Cottage at the road junction. Go over two fields by the left boundary, turning left by a barn, then by the right boundary along an avenue of trees to a road. Turn right for $^3/_4$ mile, and pass St Mary's Church, Fretherne, to a footpath on the left. Go through two fields to **Hock Cliff**.

Keeping the river on the right veer left at lock gates over a footbridge and stile and go directly across two fields diagonally, along a grassy lane, through a copse and a field to Saul Lodge. Turn left to the road, and cross the canal bridge for the Cider House Café. Continue to **Frampton-on-Severn**, turning right at the Bell pub and passing the Three Horseshoes to St Mary's lych gate and a footpath through the field to the church. Pass a kissing gate and proceed to the next stile. Go over a footbridge by the canal traffic lights. Turn left.

Cross the canal and turn left for 2 miles. At the second bridge recross the canal, pass the Tudor Arms to a bend in the road, turn right through the gate, then diagonally over the field to a footbridge in the far corner. Again go diagonally to a stile. Turn right in Lightenbrook Lane, and left over a footbridge. Keep on high ground across the field, then pass a wind pump to an electricity pole. Proceed over fields and stiles to Slimbridge churchyard, and follow the path around to a kissing gate into a field. Go diagonally to a gate in the corner. Keep the same direction, cutting off the left corner of the next field, and go across the following field to the hedge corner. Hold the left boundary to a stile, then the right boundary to a road. Ascend opposite, over a bridge, and then, with the dyke on your left, cross two fields, ditches and a bridge. Negotiate the next fields in the following way: beside the right boundary in the first and second, over Nebrow Hill in the third, by the left boundary in the fourth, the right boundary in the fifth, the left boundary in the sixth, diagonally towards a barn in the seventh, and diagonally towards a church in the eighth. Go over a fence at step-stones between some farm buildings to the road. Turn left to return to Splatt Bridge.

POINTS OF INTEREST:

Frampton-on-Severn – Claims to have the largest village green in England. Local cider is for sale in the Post Office.

Hock Cliff – A vantage point for bird watching. At high tide you can witness a fast filling of the estuary which builds up into the 'Severn Bore' as the estuary narrows.

REFRESHMENTS:
The Three Horseshoes Inn, Frampton (tel no: 0452 740463).
The Bell Inn, Frampton (tel no: 0452 740346).
Cider House Café, Frampton (tel no: 0452 741302).
The Tudor Arms, Slimbridge (tel no: 045389 306).

Walk 90   HAILEY WOOD AND COATES   4m (5km)

Maps: OS Sheets Landranger 163; Pathfinder SO 80/90 and ST 89/99.

A walk through woodland and by the towpath of a derelict canal.

Start: At 961020, just off the A419 on the Sapperton road.

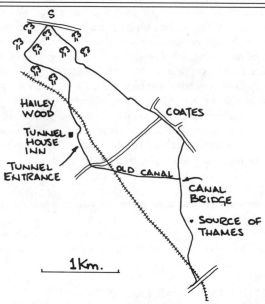

On the south side of the A419, 100 yards east of the start, opposite Four-Mile Lodge, is a stile. From the stile a broad track heads south-west, at first along the edge of the woodland. Follow this for 600 yards then turn left at a cross. Keep to the path through Hailey Wood, at one place passing underneath a railway bridge. Immediately beyond bear left and walk parallel to the railway until the **Tunnel House** pub can be seen to the right. You are now by the southern end of the **Thames and Severn Canal Tunnel**. Move slightly right and descend to the towpath on the right-hand side of the canal. Walking the towpath you will, after 1 mile, reach a stone bridge. From here you can visit the source of the Thames (see below).

If you simply want to continue the walk, turn left over the bridge, and after a few yards walk up the side of a field with a stone wall to your right. At the top of the field cross a small stone stile and walk up the next field with a stone wall to your left. Another stone stile is your exit to a road, along which you go left for $^1/_2$ mile. Where the road bends right go straight on along a narrow path. Cross the churchyard, and after the gate, walk left for a few yards, turning right beyond a house. Advancing between fences for a short distance you soon enter a field and hug the left-hand boundary. A gate gives access to a further field, at the far end of which it is possible to go left to join a path inside a wood.

You should now follow the yellow arrows that guide the walker round a saw mill complex. This includes going left from the path you have just joined then right at a T-junction. You eventually arrive at a large clearing with saw mill buildings to the right (it can be very muddy here). Turn left along a broad track, but after $^1/_4$ mile go right. In 100 yards you will arrive at the stile that you crossed to the begin the walk.

The traditional source of the Thames is little more than $^1/_4$ mile from the stone bridge. There is no water there now and even the stone figure of Father Thames has been moved to Lechlade. To visit you should go right (instead of crossing the bridge) and enter a field by a gate. Cross the field and go over a stile beside another gate. The site is then a few yards to the left.

It is also possible to visit the Thames Head Inn for a meal or some other refreshment. To do so, continue in the same line through two further gates and then go slightly right to another gate. A track can now be seen ascending slightly to the railway line. Cross the stile and, exercising care, go over the railway to a further stile. Now go left, parallel with the railway, until a gate gives access to the A429. The Thames Head Inn is a few yards away to the right.

POINTS OF INTEREST:

Tunnel House Inn – Built to accommodate the workers on the canal tunnel.
The Thames and Severn Canal Tunnel – Built between 1784 and 1789, 3817 yards long. At its opening date, the longest in existence.

REFRESHMENTS:

Tunnel House Inn (tel no: 028577 280). Bar meals available.
Thames Head Inn (tel no: 028577 259). Bar meals available.

Walk 91   ABLINGTON AND CALCOT CIRCULAR   4½m (7km)

Maps: OS Sheets Landranger 163; Pathfinder SP 00/10 & 01/11.
A walk on downland track, footpath and country lane, visiting four villages in the valley of the River Coln.
Start: At 102077, Ablington Mill.

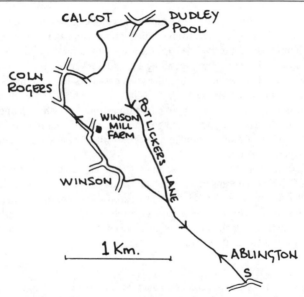

Take the broad drive alongside the Mill (now private residences) in a north-westerly direction, with the river on your left and cottages on the right above you. Go through a wooden gate and stay on the track as it skirts a walled enclosure on the left. Go across a grassy valley and climb a steep bank. After the gate at the top of the rise bear half-left on an indistinct path across the field, making for the far left-hand corner where there is a gate concealed in the hedge. Follow the footpath between the belt of woodland on the left and the fence on the right, going left and downhill through the wood at a point opposite a gate in the right-hand fence. When clear of the wood the path goes across a flat, sometimes marshy, meadow to a footbridge over the Coln. Go through two white wicket gates to a lane. Turn right into Winson village. Pass a telephone kiosk and go straight over the crossing lanes, up the hill. Just beyond Village Farm take the right-hand road towards Coln Rogers. Shortly you will pass Winson Mill on the left. Cross the Coln once more and immediately turn left opposite the entrance to Winson Mill Farm, one-time home of the author Robert Henriques. Approaching **Coln Rogers** you cross over Swains Bridge and then turn right through the village.

Take the first turning right after the telephone kiosk, down a lane signed 'To the Saxon Church', passing the church on your left.Go straight on until the lane goes over a bridge into the private gardens of Pigeon House. Here, take the track to the left, over a bridge and go immediately left on to a footpath leading along the river bank and through The Grove. Emerge from the wood and go across the water meadow to a farm gate just below the village houses ahead of you. Turn right to walk uphill through Calcot village. Go straight over the crossroads at the top and then fork right, opposite some barns, on to a broad track known as Dudley. At a T-junction by some semi-derelict farm buildings, turn right, and when meeting a metalled road turn sharp left into the track called Potlickers Lane. This is a medieval road which has deteriorated into a farm track. Stay on the track between hedges, but when it goes left, go straight on through the farm gate into a field and keep to the left-hand wall. After the next gate, when the track reappears, you can follow it back to **Ablington** and your car.

POINTS OF INTEREST:
Coln Rogers – St Andrew's Church is Anglo-Saxon.
Ablington – The Tudor Manor was once the home of Arthur Gibb, author of the classic work *A Cotswold Village* .

REFRESHMENTS:
The Catherine Wheel, Arlington, Bibury (tel no: 028574 250).
The Hare and Hounds, Fosse Cross (tel no: 028572 288).

Walk 92   FAIRFORD RIVER WALK   4½m (7km)

Maps: OS Sheets Landranger 163; Pathfinder SP 00/10.

A walk by the River Coln. Full of interest, especially for ornithologists.

Start: Fairford Church.

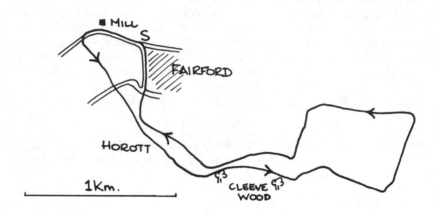

Go to the nearby T-junction and turn left into Mill Lane. Proceed ahead and down to the **River Coln**, passing a lovely house on the right. Cross the river and look for a stone stile in the wall on the left after 100 yards. Go over and straight across the field beside a small stream and individual trees. Arriving by the houses opposite go over two stiles and into a road. Cross the road to Waterloo Lane. Continue ahead to the 'Cycling Prohibited' sign and go on to a path beside a soccer pitch. At the end of the field where a wooden fence (left) and a stone wall (right) begin, go left on to a minor path at the back of a house. Follow the path round and go over a stile across a rough field with a high wall on the right. Notice the weather vane of a horse rider on a nearby house.

    Continue ahead to a farm, turn left through a white gate at the entrance and then turn right and make a line for the cottage ahead. Cross the gravel parking place and go ahead to a footbridge and stile, and into a field. Following the track, go left, getting near to the hedge, pass through a gate and follow the hedge on the right. Passing a solitary gatepost, veer left under the power cables to a gate in a wooded area. Go over a footbridge and through scrub and then cross a second bridge over the River Coln. Turn left and go over another bridge into an open area. Follow the yellow waymarks to the right and keep near the hedge. Go round to some contractors' buildings. Follow the edge of the gravel pit on the left, then go ahead in line with the electric cables on the track to the top of the gravel pit near a road. At this point go left across the grassy area and make a line for a facing hedge that sticks out. Pass this and in 175 yards take a path between hedges. Emerging from this by an old railway line, turn left with a hedge on the right and continue ahead. At the end of the pond go right over a bridge to be by the river. Follow the River Coln bank for four fields and then pass along the back of some houses. Continue on and go through a wicket gate on to a path which leads to a road that reaches **Fairford** by the White Hart. The church where you started is straight ahead.

POINTS OF INTEREST:

Fairford – The church of St Mary's is a must for any visitor to this village. Twenty-eight of the windows are of 15th-century glass – 2000 square feet of the very finest quality – and were used to express and teach the Christian faith.

The River Coln – Full of interest, while the disused gravel pits support hundreds of waterfowl. We saw over 100 Canada geese and a heron on the day we visited Fairford.

REFRESHMENTS:
Numerous in Fairford.

Walk 93   MISERDEN PARK   5¹/₄m (8.5km)

Maps: OS Sheets Landranger 163; Pathfinder SO 80/90.

A varied walk, partly in parkland, partly across fields.

Start: At 933089, the car park near Miserden village school.

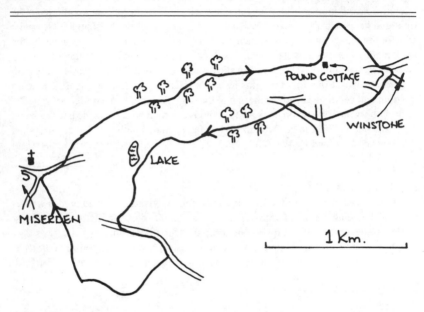

Go past **Miserden Church** to where a tree marks the centre of the village and, bearing slightly left, start down the slope. A white gate can be seen ahead and to the left. Go through the pedestrian gate alongside it and follow the metalled drive until confronted by a large tree. Now bear slightly right and aim for the stone stile below and at the edge of a wooded area. Cross the stile and enter the trees, keeping in the same line. The path descends to a junction of metalled ways. Follow the further one, still maintaining the line as it crosses a stone bridge and starts to ascend Winstone Hill. Where the drive bends sharply right, keep straight on (the path is rather indistinct). Arriving at a cross-track turn left for about 40 yards, then strike up right by a large beech tree. The path is barely discernible, but in a short time you reach a splendid stone stile at the top end of the slope. This is the edge of the park and you should now aim across the level field towards a gate with a footpath sign by it, to gain the road.

Go right along the road for a few yards to another footpath sign on the left side. There is another stone stile in the wall at this point. From here take a line almost parallel with the left-hand field boundary and 30-40 yards from it until you encounter the boundary where it juts out. Follow the boundary to another irregularity, then aim for a gate by Pound Cottage. Going through the gate, turn left along a broad track for 300 yards to a footpath sign on the right. Gaining access to the field by a stone stile, cross it to the opposite corner. Turn left for 30 yards along the road then go right along a path. This is Winstone village and you will soon arrive at a junction of metalled roads. Go straight over to a footpath sign and cross a wire fence. Two consecutive fields are now traversed corner to corner, to reach Gaskills Farm. Turn half-right along a public road (ignoring a sharper right-hand turn) and go to a further junction where a drive between trees can be seen on the left.

Follow the drive for $^1/_2$ mile, until it turns right. Keep straight on down a track marked 'Bridleway'. Keep going down (very muddy at times) to the lake in the valley bottom. Walk along the lake embankment and turn left, taking the wide track up the slope. Where it levels slightly, bear right, still ascending, until a metalled lane is reached. Now go left down the lane for a little more than $^1/_4$ mile. It bottoms then rises for a few yards. At the top of the rise there is a gate to the right. Go through and straight up the field to another gate at the left-hand end of a small copse. Go through this and in a few yards join a wide track along the top edge of the trees. Eventually it veers left. Keep with it but after 100 yards turn right along a field boundary with the wall to your left. After another $^1/_4$ mile you will reach the lane again, but go straight across and along a further field with the wall now to your right. A final stile gives access to a track that leads into Miserden village.

POINTS OF INTEREST:

Miserden Church –The built-up north doorway has a Saxon arch and there is a Saxon doorway in the 13th-century porch. There is also a magnificent tomb with alabaster figures of Sir William and Margaret Sandys.

REFRESHMENTS:

The Carpenters Arms (tel no: 028582 283). Bar meals available.

Walk 94 THE AMPNEYS 6m (9.5km)

Maps: OS Sheets Landranger 163; Pathfinder SP 00/10.

A level walk, half in meadowland and half on lanes through pretty villages.

Start: At 073017, in the loop road, Ampney Crucis.

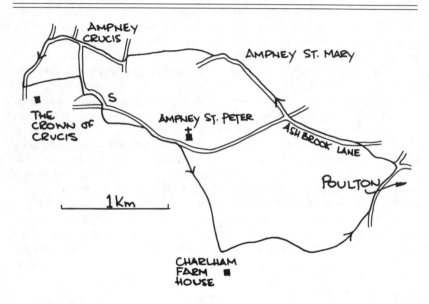

Leave the loop road at its eastern end, cross the main road, turn right over Ampney Brook and immediately left into a field. Follow the stream to a footbridge which you cross to visit **St Mary's Church**, afterwards going through the churchyard to regain the road, and turn right. Walk on the wide right-hand verge and turn right on to a metalled track between the bus shelter and a telephone kiosk. Proceed for about $^3/_4$ mile on the lane and then go left on to a bridle path just before you reach Charlham Farm House. In 600 yards another bridle path goes off at right-angles, and at this point you go half-right through two fields on an occasionally obscured footpath, steering slightly to the right of a wind pump just visible beyond the trees ahead. At the copse go right for a few yards, then over a footbridge on your left to follow a footpath straight ahead through the trees and enter a field by a farm gate. Here, go half-left, over a stile into the sports ground, making for the distinctive bell tower of the church of St Michael and All the Angels. Note the crosses carved out of live trees in the churchyard.

Turn left on the road into Poulton and straight on, passing The Falcon Inn and the Post Office on your right, to a T-junction with Bell Lane going straight ahead. Do not enter Bell Lane, but turn left into a very narrow path by the side of a house named The New Inn. Go over a stile into a field. Again the path may be indistinct, but follow the direction given by the finger post at the stile as far as the middle of the field, then go half-right making for a large tree and a stone stile giving access into a track named Ashbrook Lane. Turn left on the track, straight over at the crossroads and through Ampney St Mary.

At the end of the village the lane turns sharp left and at the first field boundary beyond farm buildings on your right, enter a field and follow the hedge on the right. Go through the gateway by the side of a cattle trough and turn left. Keep the hedge on your left at first but, after negotiating the footbridge, steer straight across the large field to pass right of a plantation and the houses visible ahead. At the lane turn left then first right into **Ampney Crucis**, passing the school and Post Office on the left, and follow the descending road as it curves to the left and passes the village hall. If you wish to visit the church go on until you see the appropriate direction sign. Otherwise, look out on the left for a house boldly named Pippins, and at the end of its frontage turn left on a path which takes you through its garden, across the sports field, and over a footbridge. Here, walk straight ahead on the clear footpath leading to the left of a large house at the end of a copse ahead. Go down the track by the side of the house, and right on to a lane which will take you back to your car.

POINTS OF INTEREST:
St Mary's Church – About 12th-century. Believed to have been the parish church of Ampney St Mary, now some distance away, the original village having been decimated by the Black Death. Now isolated in a field, the church is in good repair and has a wealth of interesting features including a unique tympanum.
Ampney Crucis – Holy Rood church is of Norman origin, and has an interesting cross in the churchyard. The gardens of the Jacobean manor of Ampney Park are sometimes open to the public.

REFRESHMENTS:
The Crown of Crucis, Ampney Crucis (tel no: 028585 403).
The Butchers Arms, Ampney Crucis (tel no: 028585 486).
The Falcon Inn, Poulton (tel no: 028585 392).

Walk 95   SOUTH CERNEY   6m (9.5km)

Maps: OS Sheets Landranger 163; Pathfinder SU 09/19.

A superb walk around the Cotswold Water Park.

Start: At 073972, the parking area 400 yards south-west down the Spine Road entering the park from the A419.

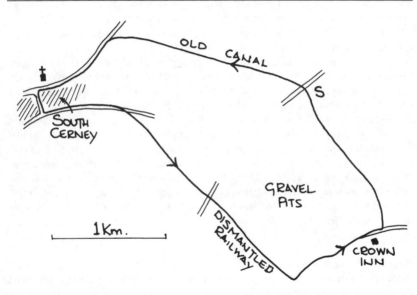

Start out from the north-west corner of the **Water Park** car park. Cross the road to a stile beside the old canal and go forward to an old ruin on the right. Continue ahead following the canal on the right for about 1 mile to a road. Turn left on to the road (oddly named 'Bow Wow'), cross over the old railway bridge and walk along to South Cerney, with the church and, in a garden, a small tower on your right. At the road bridge – which has a rather unusual arrangement – over the River Churn, turn left past the Old George Inn. Walk to the main road, Station Road, turn left and, leaving the village, follow the fence on the right. Where the fence runs to the right, away from the road, follow the path alongside it. Now, with water on your right, continue ahead past the boating area to arrive at a car park by a red-brick bridge.

Go under the bridge, across the main road, and through a gate to follow a bridleway. In under 1 mile (when a bridge and a black and white arrow come into sight ahead) look for a path left to Cerney Wick Lakes. Go over a stile (there is a white chimney straight ahead) and continue forward over a footbridge to come to an old gravel pit. Follow the path round to the right for about 500 yards and where the path bends back up north-west look for a stile in the right corner. Continue ahead over stiles to the road, cross over and go on to another road by the Crown Inn. In Cerney Wick walk along the road to the bridge over a canal and take the path left, marked 'South Cerney 2 miles'.

There is a lovely roundhouse here and plenty of evidence of the planned restoration of the canal. Continue ahead and when you pass over a concrete footbridge you take the path left across a field back to your starting point.

POINTS OF INTEREST:
The Cotswold Water Park – Still being developed. The old gravel pits attract all kinds of water sports, and there are plenty of waterfowl to see too.

REFRESHMENTS:
The Old George, South Cerney (tel no: 0285 860333).
The Crown Inn, Cerney Wick (tel no: 0793 780369).

Walk 96   COLN ST ALDWYN AND BIBURY   6m (9.5km)

Maps: OS Sheets Landranger 163; Pathfinder SP 00/10.

A ramble across hills to Bibury, returning along the river.

Start: At 144047, on the river bridge between Coln St Aldwyn and Quenington.

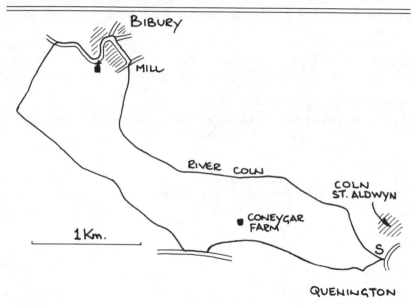

From the river bridge go through the gates by the lodge and head straight up the bank away from the river. Follow the track to the gate at the top by a wood, pass through and go ahead to a facing wall and, keeping the wall on the left, cross a field to a gate. Continue ahead and make for an old cottage as you cross the field to a gate. Pass between the cottage and Coneygar Farm. Go through a gate and across a field towards a house at the far end. Pass through the gate on to a road, turn right passing a house and in 150 yards turn right on to a bridleway. Go down to a gate and into a field. Go down to the bottom, through a gate and climb the track beside a wood on the left. Go up into a field and, with the hedge on your right, continue to the next gate. With a hedge on your left in the next field go to the next gate and after 120 yards take a good track on the right to **Bibury**.

With the remains of a wall and hawthorn on the left, continue ahead, through a wicket gate where five footpaths are marked. Continue ahead across the field through a gate and past a house. Go down to the road and turn right to the famous Arlington Row of cottages. Pass in front of these and go over the bridge to the road. Turn right and follow the river (plenty of trout and ducks to see). At the point where the road turns left uphill go right, down to the church, and then follow the path round and up to the telephone box. Go on to the main road, turn right and follow the road round and up to the right turn for Coln St Aldwyns. Go along this road, and in 50 yards turn right to a mill. Walk between the buildings and up the slope. Go through a gate, left, on to a track across water meadows, through the next gate, up a slope and turn left at the top. Follow the wood on the left and keep left at the fork to cross a field. Go through wicket gates, down a bank and into the next field. Cross this to a wooded area, pass through and continue ahead following the track beside the River Coln. You cross fields and go through a wood and then another field on your way back to the start of the walk.

POINTS OF INTEREST:
Bibury – A well-known Cotswold village beside the Coln. Well worth a walk around.

REFRESHMENTS:
Numerous in Bibury.

Walk 97   COLN VALLEY CIRCULAR   7m (11km)

Maps: OS Sheets Landranger 163; Pathfinder SP 01/11.
Woodland, village, parkland and River Coln. Best in late spring.
Start: At 053134, The Chedworth Roman Villa.

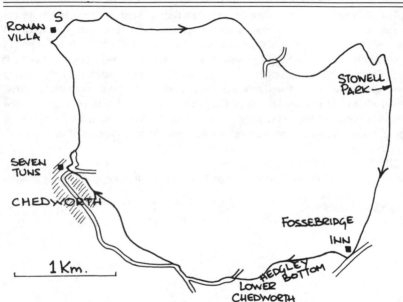

From the **Roman Villa**, go down the metalled lane and turn right at the minor
crossroads into the private road. Stay on this, alongside the River Coln, until you
emerge from the wood. Go first left and, opposite Yanworth Mill, right through a
hunting gate to walk through three fields keeping to their right-hand boundaries. Upon
reaching a road, turn right immediately, through a gate, and walk across the field,
paralle! with a line of hawthorns and a brook on your left, to a gate and the road again.
Turn left for a few yards and then right through a gate by a cottage. Walk south on a
path with a view of Stowell Park, left. Go through a gate and turn right along a wall.
Go through another gate and straight on with a copse to the right. After the next gate
go up to more woodland, skirting it to the right, then through a gate on your left to turn
right and follow a concrete track through a wood and the remains of a war-time camp.
    When you meet a crossing concrete road go straight ahead on a footpath through

the wood, downhill all the way, and after emerging into a field bear slightly left towards a park wall, down a steep bank to the Fosse Way (A429). Turn right on this dangerous road keeping on the right-hand footpath. Go past the Fossebridge Inn and, just past the first house beyond the first road on your right, turn right on to a track. Follow this as it veers left along Hedgeley Bottom to meet a road in lower **Chedworth**. Turn left along the road and, just after the crest of the hill beyond the telephone kiosk, look out for a house on the right named Saffron Hill. Here the choice is yours. If you prefer you can keep on the road through the village, to admire the old houses and gardens on the way to The Seven Tuns pub. Otherwise, turn right down the grassy drive by the side of Saffron Hill and go over a stile on the left just before entering the private garden. Follow the distinct footpath over five fields to a minor road, where you go right for about 50 yards to Brook Cottage. Exactly opposite the cottage cross the stone stile to walk along the valley bottom, over a series of stiles, until you meet a Cotswold stone wall at right-angles. Here, go left to a stile in the top left-hand corner of the field and cross the disused railway embankment. On the other side go half-right through a gate and across a paddock, keeping to the upper boundary, to a stile which gives access to a short footpath between hedges leading to the road by the side of The Seven Tuns . Suitably refreshed, go up the sunken footpath opposite the pub to the church, turn right in front of cottages on a footpath signed to the Roman villa, and go over a stile. Follow the footpath to the left, making for a broken stile near the right-hand end of the wall surrounding the wood ahead. Go through the tip of the wood, bearing right to cross a stone stile into a field, then straight ahead to pass through a hunting gate into another field. Here keep to the right-hand wall heading for woodland, and when the wall/fence ends, merge with a well-used track leading to a stile into Chedworth Woods. Just inside the wood take the left fork, following a broad track until you come to a crossing where the right-hand track is signposted downhill to the Roman villa. Follow this track, under the old railway bridge to return to your car.

POINTS OF INTEREST:
The Roman Villa – National Trust property. Mosaics, hypercausts and a museum. Said to have been found in the last century by a gamekeeper digging out a lost ferret! **Chedworth** – The village has many attractive cottages. St Andrew's Church is in Norman and Perpendicular style.

REFRESHMENTS:
The Fossebridge Inn, Fossebridge (tel no: 028572 721).
The Seven Tuns Pub, Chedworth (tel no: 028572 242).

Walk 98   SAPPERTON   8m (13km)

Maps: OS Sheets Landranger 163; Pathfinder SO 80/90.

A fairly level walk through woods. Muddy in parts.

Start: At 910019, the car park at Cowcombe Hill lay-by on the A419.

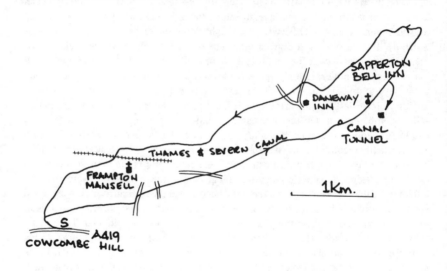

Walk down the lane at the end of the car park and turn right through the first gate, along a bridle path beside a wall. At a minor road, turn left for 100 yards and right along a footpath with a wall on the left. Cross a minor road, two large fields and continue with a coppice on the left and a wall on the right until you descend eight wooden steps to a road. Turn left along the road for 200 yards and turn sharp right along a footpath in a wood, forking right a few yards before a huge ventilation shaft from a railway tunnel. Follow this muddy cart-track to the road between Sapperton and Daneway. Cross the road and continue along the cart-track, forking left to reach the entrance of the canal tunnel. Turn right to go over the top of the tunnel to a stile. Walk across the field towards **Sapperton Church** and climb the stile to a footpath with barbed wire on the left.

Cross the road and ascend a walkway to another road. Turn left and at the road junction take the bridle path leaving the church below on the left. Traverse five fields and enter a short wood, emerging into a very large field. At the end of this, fork left and then turn left down a muddy track. Step across a small stream and ascend the path opposite, going up steeply between high banks. At the top, where four tracks meet, turn left along a muddy track, which, after 1 mile, meets a road by Daneway House. Here, unless you wish to visit the Daneway Inn, cross the road and take the footpath contouring across a field to another minor road. Cross this and enter **Siccaridge Wood Nature Reserve**.

After $^1/_2$ mile, when the track turns sharp right, look for a footpath, half-left, going south and downhill, gently at first and then steeply to a bridge across the canal. Cross this and turn right to follow the canal to another bridge, after which the dirt road swings away from the canal to go under a railway viaduct to Manor House. Turn right up the road, left up the bridle path and immediately right up a footpath which starts by a barbed wire fence. The path swings away left to a field gate and squeezer, and then contours round below trees. Follow the cart-track to Westley Farm and continue along the minor road back to the car park.

POINTS OF INTEREST:

The Severn-Thames Canal – Now derelict, was used between 1789 and 1909 and the Sapperton Canal Tunnel, which is $2^1/_4$ miles long, was opened by George III.

Sapperton Church – Has some beautiful wooden pew carvings here and interesting statues.

Siccaridge Wood Nature Reserve – There are extensive patches of lily-of-the-valley in the Reserve.

REFRESHMENTS:

The Bell Inn, Sapperton (tel no: 028576 298).

The Daneway, Sapperton (tel no: 028576 297).

The White Horse Inn, Sapperton (tel no: 028576 279).

Walk 99   COLN ST ALDWYN AND HATHEROP   8m (13km)

Maps: OS Sheets Landranger 163; Pathfinder SP 00/10.

An interesting walk by the river and through Cotswold villages.
Start: At 144047, on the river bridge between Coln St Aldwyn
and Quenington.

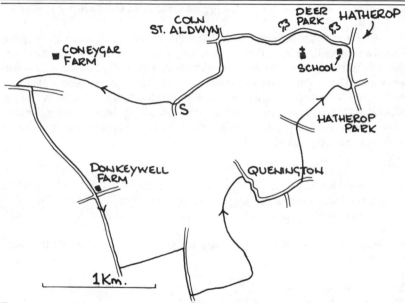

From the river bridge go through the gates by the lodge and head straight up the bank,
away from the river. Follow the track to the gate at the top by a wood, pass through, go
ahead to a facing wall and, keeping the wall left, cross a field to a gate. Continue ahead
and make for an old cottage as you cross the field to a gate. Pass through between the
cottage and Coneygar Farm. Go through a gate and cross the field to a house at the far
end. Pass through the gate on to a road, turn left, go forward 150 yards and then turn
right on to a narrow road between trees. Stay on this road to Donkeywell Farm. Cross
over the road by the farm on to a concrete road down to houses. Continue ahead down
the track to a field and walk to the bottom of the field with a hedge on your left. Turn
left on to a definite track and make for the wind pump by the road. At the road turn right,
go forward for 400 yards and turn left through a gate on to a track with a wood on the

right. Go to the bottom of the field, through a gate with a fence on the right and proceed ahead up the field with views of the river to the right. The fence gives way to a hedge which you follow, but now look for a gap (by a 'No Admittance' notice) to pass through. Go down the bank and into a wooded area through a pull-apart stile and into a field. Follow a wall and the wood on your left and walk round to a gate. Pass through and follow the wooden fence on your right to another gate. Continue ahead to the road and into **Quenington**. Have a walk round the village if you have the time, and investigate the Keeper's Arms and the Earl Grey up on the left for refreshments.

To continue the walk, turn down the road past the church, cross over the river and go up the slope to where the road bears right. Take the farm track left and where it turns right up to Leafield Farm continue ahead through a single metal gate and on to the road. At the road cross over into Hatherop Park and follow the track and paths to arrive at the road on the far side. Turn left to **Hatherop**. Continue along the road and take the left turning to Coln St Aldwyn. Pass a school and telephone box and, if you wish to visit the church, go through a stone-roofed gateway opposite Sandpiper Cottage. Proceed on down the road passing Hatherop Castle School on the left. At the bottom by the river it is worth a few minutes to detour left and see the work being done on the weirs and the unusual wooden water tank. Return to the road and continue forward past Williamstrip Deer Park and on to **Coln St Aldwyn**. Turn left at the crossroads and follow the road down to the river and the start of the walk.

POINTS OF INTEREST:

Quenington – The 12th-century church is worth a visit. The tympanum over the south doorway depicts the Coronation of the Virgin while that over the north doorway with its timbered porch depicts the harrowing of Hell. In the nearby court is a round dovecote. The nearby gatehouse formed part of buildings which belonged to Knights Hospitallers.

Hatherop – The church and castle.

Coln St Aldwyn – Its church and almshouses.

REFRESHMENTS:

The Keepers Arms, Quenington (tel no: 028575 349).

The Earl Grey, Quenington (tel no: 028575 483).

Walk 100 THE DUNTISBOURNES AND EDGEWORTH 9m (14.5km)
Maps: OS Sheets Landranger 163; Pathfinder SO 80/90.
A walk mostly through fields but in varied surroundings.
Start: At 968078, to the south-west of Duntisbourne Abbots.

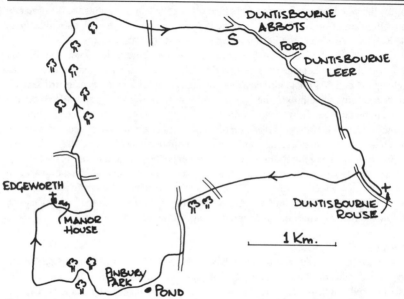

Go towards the village and turn right to pass the churchyard. Go right again by the telephone box and in a short time you will come to Duntisbourne's celebrated ford where the lane becomes the course of the brook for about 70 yards. There is a footpath along the right-hand side. At a T-junction turn right (less than 100 yards to the left is another picturesque ford) and, shortly, left. Inside 200 yards bear right along a lane that is at first unfenced. At a place where the road dips, go left along a level path and then left again where it gives on to a road. In a very few yards go right on a footpath just past the first building and aim for a point where a fence sticks out from the left. Now proceed down the centre of the main field (path indistinct here) and as it narrows go towards the bottom corner near the brook where the track can be seen. Cross the stile and climb obliquely across the bank. Soon you will emerge by the quaint little church of **Duntisbourne Rouse**. Enter the churchyard and go right through an unusual gate.

Emerging on to the lane turn right. At about 300 yards go left on an obvious track and after a similar distance bear right, ignoring the gate straight ahead. Follow this track (can be muddy) and where it meets the road to Daglingworth go straight across in the same line. You will see a sign to Pinbury Park. Turn right along the drive – although the sign says 'Private' this is a public bridleway. It winds down, passing to the right of a pond and then to the left of the houses of Pinbury. Soon you will arrive at a ford on the River Frome, with a footbridge to the right. The track now ascends steeply up the edge of woodland and emerges at a gate. Go up the right-hand boundary of a field to a prominent group of trees known as Gloucester Beeches. A stile enables you to turn right and you go across a series of fields keeping to their right-hand boundaries. After three fields the ground drops away and you will see the village of Edgeworth ahead. Go over the stile and aim for a cottage with four small gables along its main roof. A gate here gives access to a lane which in a short distance 'tees' into another lane almost opposite the church. Turn right towards the gates to **Edgeworth Manor** but go right again through an iron gate between stone pillars to gain a driveway. This drive, which is also a bridle path, takes you down below the Manor House and descends to cross the Frome by a stone bridge. Go through a gate and follow the drive out to the road where you bear left to re-cross the river and ascend steeply for 100 yards to an entrance to the right, signposted 'Valley Farm'. Walk along the metalled driveway to a cattle grid, leave it to the right (gate) and progress through a field to another gate. You can now see Valley Farm to the left and half-way across the near field. Go left to a gate opposite a newish-looking bungalow and, through the gate, go right immediately along a driveway to a shed. Here you can descend to the right to a stile beyond which stepping stones offer another crossing of the Frome.

Follow the track, going through another gate until a road can be seen ahead. Just short of this turn right to ascend a deeply-cut track with a tree to the right, passing under electric cables. Little more than 100 yards beyond another gate, ignore a right-hand branch, going ahead for 50 yards and forking right between two woods. At the top, pass between stone gate posts to gain a track that presently passes through sheep pens. Pass over a public road and walk along a track back to your car.

POINTS OF INTEREST:

Duntisbourne Rouse – The delightful little church with a saddleback tower has much Saxon walling: note the herringboning. Most of the remainder is Norman. It is one of the few village churches with a crypt. A medieval cross stands in the churchyard.

Edgeworth Manor – Fine 17th-century manor house, also known as Ebworth Manor.